MANAGING GOD'S FINANCES

DR. DONALD A. NURSE

Managing God's Finances

By

Dr. Donald A. Nurse, Ed.D, PCC

Abundant Life Institute
4151 Route 130 South, Edgewater Park, New Jersey 08010

MANAGING GOD'S FINANCES

May the Holy Spirit grant you wisdom in all your financial affairs. Love - Dr. D.A.N. 2/1/13

Managing God's Finances

Scripture quotations are from the Authorized King James version of the Bible (KJV)

Cover design by Jamel Browne: A depiction of the truth; "All wealth belongs to God – we are His stewards, managing His wealth through obedience to His written Word."

Registered with the IP Rights Office – September 10, 2012
Copyright Registration Service Ref: 2308490965
CreateSpace ISBN – 13:978-1479289059

Printed in the United States of America

MANAGING GOD'S FINANCES

ACKNOWLEDGEMENT

The contents of this book represent a bold endeavor to chronicle personal thoughts on Biblical financial principles. They are borne from various spiritual, practical, and academic experiences that continue to affect my life to this day. None of this would have been possible in the absence of a praying mother, a considerate and patient wife, and the many encouraging brothers and sisters of Abundant Life Fellowship Church. I am deeply grateful, and remain indebted to God for His demonstration of love shown through those mentioned above. May this work serve to justify your faith and confidence in me.
Dr. D.A.N

Abundant Life Institute
4151 Route 130 South, Edgewater Park, New Jersey 08010

MANAGING GOD'S FINANCES

Foreword

God is owner. I am manager. How often have we heard these words? The fact remains that this is true for every believer who endeavors to *"Live by the Word" of God."*

Again, Rev. Dr. Donald A. Nurse has given to us a reasoned discourse on how to order our lives by the word of God – this time in the area of finances. Many have devoured his thoughts on this very pertinent topic throughout the years, and have found them to be very helpful in managing the Lord's finances which He has so graciously entrusted to us as stewards.

Prepare yourself to be instructed, challenged, educated, and delighted, as this man of God leads you into financial freedom.

Follow the instructions contained in this book faithfully, and you will arrive at a destination that will result in much joy and satisfaction as you order your finances according to the principles of the word of God.

Dr. Nurse is to be greatly commended for his fine scholarship on this topic, and in presenting this wonderful word to the people of God.

Thank you, sir!

Rev. Dr. Eve Lynne Fenton
Abundant Life Fellowship Church
Edgewater Park, New Jersey 08010

MANAGING GOD'S FINANCES

INTRODUCTION

In the Beginning there was no End – as a matter of fact, there was no Beginning before Creation. The Beginning and the End are both elements to measure Time. Time itself is simply a created gauge to enable an understanding of the sequence of events contained in God's plan for His creation – we came from Eternity, and will return to Eternity, a place where Time does not exist. The interesting consideration is, "What happens in Time leading up to our return to Eternity?" This book has a bias toward financial issues from a Biblical perspective. However, there is no way to understand the Kingdom principles governing the management of God's resources without a clear understanding of His plan for those resources. Toward that end, this discussion is separated into two main parts – the first includes a discussion of God's plan from a historical and prophetic viewpoint, and seeks to answer the question 'Why do we need to manage God's finances?" The second part addresses the practical method/s that would enable the satisfactory management of those resources.

The global economy continues to cause a headache to the financial gurus. But are the events which are responsible for this position a manipulation by the human factor, or are they the result of natural phenomena? What explanations, if any, are available to the inquiring mind? More importantly, how should I react as a Christian? Does the Bible speak of these things? I attempt to answer some of these questions in the following pages.

The various topics are streamlined in such a way that one leads right into the other. It is meant to unfold like a story – with a Beginning and an End. However, the truths which are shared should not be viewed as a panacea for our financial ills. They should rather be seen as encouragement to pursue a greater understanding of our individual Christian roles in these End-Times.

We must understand how this world's economy operates if we are to fully appreciate how the 'system' is using money to enslave unsuspecting clients. A topic such as "A History of Banking in the U.S.A.' may appear secular in content, but really represents a spring board from which we can dive into a pool of knowledge for our benefit, and for the glory of God.

Apart from our relationship with God, money is the single element that serves our basic needs of existence in this world. There is therefore no wonder that the devil uses it to corrupt those who are gullible. It is also a feasible anticipation that money will be used as a medium to herald in the antichrist. Perhaps this latter statement signifies our need to be aware of money matters, since our very lives may depend on an understanding of such issues. The devil is a deceiver. Is it conceivable that he will be overt in his approach to have us receive the 'Mark?' I don't think so. But there are events, currently occurring in the financial and other arenas, which seem to be setting the stage for a casual acceptance of this Doomsday instrument. The topic, 'Moving Towards a Cashless Society – The Dangers,' addresses this issue.

Once we appreciate the seriousness of the times we live in, we should make every effort to appropriate the covenant promises of our Heavenly Father. Our first goal should therefore be to become totally debt free. Only then would we be in position to take our places in this phase of God's overall plan – bringing in the 'Harvest.' The latter part of this work is therefore designed to introduce various secular (but Godly) and Biblical approaches toward financial emancipation.

I have made a conscious effort to refrain from technical financial jargon when addressing financial institutions and strategies. The aim is to present the material for everyone to digest with ease. I trust therefore, that you will find the contents of the following pages both stimulating and spiritually rewarding. Let us endeavor to enforce together the victory Jesus achieved at Calvary. To God be the Glory.

Dr. D.A.N

MANAGING GOD'S FINANCES

LIST OF CONTENTS

PART I

WHY MANAGE GOD'S FINANCES?

Chapters:

PART II

SOME KINGDOM METHODS TO MANAGE GOD'S FINANCES

PART I

WHY MANAGE GOD'S FINANCES?

But thou shalt remember the Lord thy God: for it is he that giveth thee power to get wealth, that he may establish his covenant which he sware unto thy fathers, as it is this day. (Deut. 8:18)

MANAGING GOD'S FINANCES

Chapter 1

IN THE BEGINNING
THE NATURE OF PROSPERITY

Main Text – Genesis 2:4-15.

Introduction

The question, "Why manage God's finances," is a significant and fundamental link to any discussion on prosperity – that is, if the intent is to prosper by utilizing God's kingdom principles. How can one manage his or her resources in an excellent way in the absence of a *vision* and *mission?* Since all resources actually belong to God (Ps. 24:1), then it would be wise to determine how your personal vision and mission fit within God's overall plan. Only then could one be capable of making sound decisions that are compatible with His will for the financial resources he has entrusted to you. The remainder of this section is therefore devoted to the capture of the essence of God's plan – from eternity through time, and back to eternity. Since the entire issue revolves around the topic of prosperity, it is fitting that the discussion should begin with a definition of this phenomenon.

Personal Notes

Prosperity – A Definition

The world defines prosperity as physical wealth – financial, military, social, and political power. But from a Biblical viewpoint, true prosperity lies in our relationship with God – to the extent that He can use His power through us to meet the needs of others. That is why, as Creator, He furnished us with every necessity from the beginning. Come with me on a journey into the Book of Genesis. Note that because of our unique position, we are able to travel mentally to and from each destination at will.

Adam's Wealth

Everything that we have today was present in the beginning. The only difference between then and now is man's innovative techniques to harness the various aspects of creation – indeed, God admonished us to take dominion over all created things (Gen. 1:26). For example, gravity and its associated laws existed with Adam. Birds defied those laws then, but it took the Wright brothers to imitate the flight of birds and usher in the age of the aircraft. All the material necessary to make an airplane existed in Adam's time, but without the knowledge to change them into a useful state, they remained just a part of nature.

Personal Notes

Here we are in Eden, awed by the magnificence of God's creation – God gave Adam everything. The question concerning his wealth is relative to the time in which he lived. There was no need for money. His task was to dress and keep the Garden of Eden (Gen. 2:15). Food was plentiful. As a vegetarian, the work he did ensured his constant supply of all the nutrients required for his daily use. His companionship with God enabled his spiritual growth and upkeep. The thought strikes us, "What would Adam do if he lived in our time?" He would definitely need money! Then, we reflect on Gen. 2:10-14. It is obvious from our own observation that Adam was immensely rich by any standard. He had:

1. Gold without measure, including 'black gold' – oil. One of the rivers flowing from Eden – Pison, encompassed areas of the Persian Gulf. No wonder there is so much turmoil and dispute in that region
2. There is also Bdellium, a type of ruby, and the onyx stone – both precious in value.

In my view, Adam had the potential to be a great businessman. Look at the river Euphrates which also flows from Eden. It extended for 1780 miles, and is the longest and most important river of Western Asia. Since God gave Adam dominion over all His earthly creations – including the Euphrates, then Adam could legally charge a fee for the use of this resource. All real estate was under his control. Adam was indeed a wealthy man.

The Lie & The Transfer

THEN HE LOST IT! We all know the story – he succumbed to his wife's persuasive ways and disobeyed God. He took his eyes off of the Creator and focused on His creation instead – Eve. Now, if you are anything like me, you would refuse to hang around Eden any longer to witness the pending disaster. You would attempt to shout, 'No, no, Adam! Don't do it. It's a dirty trick by the devil that will snare you and cause the loss of everything you cherish – it will unleash every imaginable evil into the earth." But alas, your voice cannot be heard – remember, you are just an invisible visitor and observer from the future. Further, even if you were heard, Adam at that time had no idea of evil. You would have probably sounded crazy to him. Anyway, pleasing his wife was more important than obedience to God. So, why should he listen to you, a complete stranger?

All of our thoughts are of what could have been – if only! Hindsight is 20/20. We probably would have done the same thing Adam did. This is evident from our continued disobedience to God's commands, even though we are Christians. Jeremiah 17:9 tells us that the heart is deceitful above all things, and desperately wicked: who can know it?

So we return to 2010 only to be faced with some startling information. What Adam lost was not destroyed! It is still here today, but in the wrong hands. It is believed that between 1999 and 2019, a period of twenty years, the earth will produce about $52 trillion in new wealth comprised of minerals alone. It is also estimated that 88% of all the money legally circulated by the United States mint remains unaccounted for – that reads $134 billion. As amazing as it may seem, there are more $100 bills in circulation than there are $1 – as much as sixty (60) times more. No wonder Christians have a hard time appropriating wealth, we have been going after the $1 bills, not realizing that there is really a shortage of such currency relative to $100 bills.

Personal Notes

Personal Notes

Despite the gloom and doom propagated by those who seem concerned with the population explosion, there is really an adequate supply of essential resources to sustain life. The truth is that the world can actually support all of multiplying humanity with its physical resources at a higher standard of living than anyone has experienced in the history of mankind. The problem is simply a matter of equitable distribution.

Then And Now
Distribution – The Key

According to science, matter is never destroyed – it may change its form, but it is never destroyed. The problem of inadequate finances is therefore not due to the absence of enough wealth, but rather its inequitable distribution. Every day we hear of countless episodes of starvation around the world, even right here in this opulent country. Yet, tons of food is frequently destroyed by various administrative entities, ironically, because there is a glut. This is a tool, they say, to maintain economic stability. The hunger of millions is less important – hard to believe, but true.

Christians have an option. If we truly believe that God is the Creator and owner of everything on earth (Ps. 24:1), and further, that He is our Father who loves us unconditionally, then, taking the example of the behavior of a **good** earthly father who provides for his own, we should be confident that God is capable and desirous of supplying all our needs. It is His will to give good gifts to His children (Luke 11:9-13).

All was not lost with Adam. God instituted a plan for our redemption and reconciliation, including our financial emancipation. The transference of wealth from the hands of the unrighteous to the hands of those positioned and willing to use prosperity God's way, is imminent – it must be so if we are truly living in the last of the last days (Prov. 13:22). This transfer will pave the way for the spreading of the Gospel – enabling the Word of God to be preached in all corners of the earth. Then, look up for our redemption draws near – the Lord returns in the sky, and we are translated into eternity where there is no injustice or inequality.

Conclusion

When we compare the pristine state of Adam's existence before the 'Fall' with our modern experiences, we must conclude that there is a difference between Adam's prosperity and ours. By our definition, Adam did not even have to think about prosperity – there was no one who needed his help. But our omniscient Father, in His wisdom, thought about us, and so provided everything from the beginning. **The nature of prosperity began with, and is found in God. He uses His ability and power to help us through every difficulty.** He helped Adam directly, now he works through others to prosper His saints. Eventually, like Adam, we will have no need to ponder on prosperity, for we will all be prosperous **IN HIM.** *Glory to God!*

Personal Notes

MANAGING GOD'S FINANCES

Chapter 2

GOD'S PLAN OF REDEMPTION
(From Adam One to Adam Two – A Financial Bias)

Main Text: Isaiah 52:1-10.

Personal Notes

It Is Legal

The Cross was the Court Room where the Just, through Faith, were redeemed for all Eternity. Why was redemption necessary – redeemed from what? Where did this all begin? We need to return to the Garden of Eden for the answers. There we witness Adam's betrayal of God's trust – he sold us out to the devil. Satan was propelled into a legal position as ruler of this earth's system. Consequently, he obtained the legal right over our earthly affairs. What Satan failed to acknowledge, or simply chose to ignore, was that God was omniscient, omnipotent, and omnipresent. These attributes signify that God is aware of all that occurs, and therefore has the opportunity to orchestrate things the way he sees fit. He is also all powerful, and therefore capable of enforcing what he orchestrates. Finally, He is everywhere all at the same time, enabling him to plan the outcome of all that He allows.

Since Satan gained dominion of the earth legally, then the only just way to redeem it would be through legal methods as well. Every subsequent event after the 'Fall' was geared toward the dispensation of justice at the Cross. Whereas Satan used subterfuge to gain legal authority in this world, our God honored that position, but paved the way for us to regain what Adam lost. God, in contrast to Satan, utilized just and honorable means to effect His plan.

The Main Events

In order to understand God's plan for the ages which also includes financial matters, we need to seek an understanding of His ways. There is one topic, albeit a difficult one, that in my mind generates the type of discussion which enables an understanding of our Creator. The 'Origin of Evil,' I believe, embodies all the answers to past and current economic issues, among other things. Many theologians shy away from such a discussion because of its psychological and philosophical implications. Nevertheless, I shall venture my thoughts on the subject in an effort to lend clarity to our attitude toward the efficient stewardship of God's resources.

Personal Notes

The Origin of Evil

This issue is vital to our relationship with God because it is a stumbling block to many – the very existence of evil in the world causes some people to doubt the existence of God Himself. How can a God who is supposed to be good, allow so many atrocities in the world? Theologians and philosophers have agonized over this topic for ages, and continue to do so. This difficulty was addressed in a 1779 document, *Dialogues Concerning Natural Religion.* David Hume in an examination of the issue, raised questions concerning God and the existence of evil from a logical and philosophical viewpoint. He said, "Is God willing to prevent evil, but not able? Then, is he impotent. Is he able, but not willing? Then, is he malevolent. Is he both able and willing? Whence then is evil?"[1] The underlying question is, can good and evil co-exist in a world where a good God is sovereign? The following is my position on the issue.

Eternity and Creation

According to the Bible, God is the Creator of everything that exists. We learn in Genesis 1, that He created the earth and everything within. This implies the pre-existence of God before anything was created. God, we understand, dwells in eternity – time is simply an aspect of His creation to facilitate a chronological understanding of events within His creation.

The account of creation and its immediate aftermath described in Genesis 1 through 3, leaves the impression that evil began when Eve succumbed to the deceptive advances of Satan. She had the ability to choose between remaining obedient to God, and to be content with the fruit from the *Tree of Life,* or to follow Satan's ploy and partake of the *Tree of the Knowledge of Good and Evil.* The observation at this point is that prior to eating from the latter, neither Eve nor Adam had any idea of the difference between good and evil. If God created this tree, and warned His creation against its use, then He must have known of the potential danger – He must have known the difference between these two elements that would usher in a dilemma for all humanity. It follows then, that evil came into existence either at the time the earth was created, or existed prior to this event.

Personal Notes

Our efforts to trace the origin of evil are helped by two observations. The first is found in Gen. 3, and surrounds the fact that the innocent Eve was beguiled by the crafty Satan. This in itself implies that Satan was privy to evil before advancing his strategy to gain control of this earth's system. The second lies in the words of God Himself. In Gen. 3:22 He observed that "….. the man has become as one of us, to know good and evil …" This suggests that God also had prior knowledge of evil, and takes us beyond the earth, to a signal episode in heaven.

The account of Lucifer's treason as recorded in Isa. 14:12-15 points to the first recorded act of evil and gives us a clue to the essence of the problem. Lucifer made a choice to become Satan – that is, to become God's adversary. The question remains, however, by whose standards do we judge Satan's actions as right or wrong? Who decides ultimately, what is moral or immoral, who determines what is good or evil?

There is no way to assess good in the absence of evil or vice versa. Since God is considered good, then evil must have been a consideration which embodied His own existence. The rejection of evil was a choice He made so that His nature could be wholly good. Every intelligent aspect of his creation was given the same opportunity – to make the choice between these two alternatives. Satan, Adam, and Eve all made the wrong choice.

Humanity was created in His image (Gen. 1:26). We are partakers of His divine nature (2 Pet. 1:3, 4) and therefore have the ability to choose correctly, that is, to choose good over evil. Perhaps the crowning statement was made by the

Lord Himself. In Isa. 45:6, 7. In His own words He said, *"I form the light, and create darkness: I make peace, and create evil: I the Lord do all these things."* The ultimate responsibility for the existence of evil, then, lies with God. This explosive truth was summed up by Martin Luther who expressed the opinion that *"the devil is the Lord's devil. He functions within the sovereign purposes of God to achieve the things that are in the eternal decree of God for the salvation of sinners, the damnation of sinners and the ultimate triumphant destruction over evil."*[2]

Personal Notes

In summary we can say that evil is really a choice made against all that God represents. The Creator of the universe embodied laws to govern His creation – including his created beings, angelic and human. There is a right standard that can only be judged through an understanding of who God is. It is this standard which presents a challenge to each of us, simply because He has given us the right to choose. Evil then, is a choice of action inimical to our best interests as it affects our relationship with God negatively – a rejection of God's ways. Implicit within this concept, and specific to this discussion, is that choices relative to economic issues that are contrary to sound Biblical principles, will limit our ability to manage God's finances efficiently.

The Importance of Right Choices

Decisions, decisions, decisions! Every day we need to make them for one thing or the other. This free will that God has entrusted to us demands that we make choices. While allowing us to exercise this freedom through the ages, God raised up men and women who remained faithful to Him and took the message of reconciliation to the people. Events recorded in the Old Testament indicate that God was preparing us for His Trump Card – the sacrifice of Jesus at Golgotha. A chronicle of pertinent events would capture the following:

01. Humans were so evil after the 'Fall,' that God wanted to wipe them out. But Noah came to the rescue by remaining faithful and obedient to God. When the flood came, Noah and his family were prepared, they had built

Personal Notes

the Ark under God's instructions – greater than the Titanic, it remained afloat, and so saved humanity from total extinction (Gen. 6 – 9).

02. Abraham and his journey of faith is next. Seeking the truth, he moved away from the security of his father's house – from Mesopotamia, the cradle of modern civilization according to some scholars. He changed his allegiance from idols to the one and only true God. The various trials he experienced, his triumphs and victories as a result of his faith in the Creator, all encourage us to take a serious look at our personal relationship with God (Gen. 12 – 25).

03. Next we have Joseph's government in Egypt and God's maneuver to sustain Israel. (Gen. 37 – 50)

04. This is climaxed by Israel's growth, consequent enslavement after Joseph's death, and their subsequent deliverance from Egyptian tyranny through Moses (Ex. 1 – 13).

05. Joshua then replaced Moses, and led Israel into the Promised Land where they exercised power and dominion (Book of Joshua).

06. Disobedience to God's statutes and decrees ushered in another period of decline in the history of Israel. The days of the Judges saw a fluctuation in the spiritual stability of the nation. Deborah, Gideon, Abimelech, Jephthah, and Samson, all served among others to deliver Israel from time to time. Nevertheless, they were constantly harassed by the original occupants of the land who remained – a snare to their existence because of disobedience (Book of Judges).

Personal Notes

07. At this point, God's plan takes form. The union of Boaz and Ruth heralds the continuation of Jesus' bloodline (His earthly origin can be traced back to Adam – Luke 3:23-38). Note that Ruth is a Moabite, and not a Jew – Jesus is for everyone, Jew and Gentile (Book of Ruth).

08. The military exploits of Saul and David brought Israel a resurgence of spiritual stability and prosperity (Books of Samuel).

09. Then the peace and consolidation of North and South under the monarchy of David, was enjoyed for a time during the reign of his son Solomon. This was later destroyed – once again because of disobedience (1 Kings 2 – 11).

10. The Psalms, especially those written by David, also served as a prophetic voice to alert Israel of the Messiah's coming – Jesus Himself referred to many of these Psalms, even as he suffered on the Cross.
11. The prophetic words of Isaiah and other men of God, including Daniel, Joel, Haggai, and Malachi, all served to reinforce God's plan for the ages – from Eternity to Eternity.
12. The preparation of John the Baptist for the advent of the Messiah ensured that Israel was warned once more of the need to choose the things of God over things of His adversary, Satan (The Gospel of Luke).
13. The simple faith and willingness of Mary supported by the pious acceptance of her husband Joseph, heralded the manifestation of God's ingenious plan (Gospel of Luke).
14. The nurturing and protection of young Jesus from the likes of king Herod, demonstrated the careful and meticulous way in which God set the stage for the unfolding of our redemption (Gospel of Luke).

15. Finally, Jesus' Ministry and the gathering of His disciples served to unfold the plan of redemption in its entirety, including instructions on how to manage His finances (The Gospels).

There is one significant episode in God's plan of redemption that stands out as a clear picture of His love, and clearly illustrates the impact of wrong choices – the deliverance of Israel from Egypt. Despite the risk of being repetitious or redundant, the story should be revisited although familiar to most of us. The idea is to build a firm foundation for our understanding of the intricacies of God's financial plan.

Moses – A Man for All Seasons

Before Moses, there was Joseph. We witness his rise to a position of authority in the Egyptian government. Our unique vantage point as spiritual travelers in time, allows us to view all of Joseph's trials; the doubt and envy of his family, the treachery of his brothers as they sold him into slavery, the temptation of Potiphar's wife and her reaction to his rejection, his imprisonment and release, and finally, his strategy to save Egypt from famine. We note that he's just a man, but one with uncompromising fortitude in his love and obedience to God – a man that made the right choice. It is this man that overcame all the trials and temptations he faced that God used to signal the demise of the 'System.' God will always use a faithful man or woman.

Joseph's rise to power in Egypt allowed him to provide adequately for his family (the people of Israel). He established a place for them in Goshen, a lucrative area of rural Egypt. Note, he used his wealth and power to help others – this understanding is paramount for the right perception of true prosperity, and consequently the proper management of God's finances. All of Israel was saved through one man's obedience. We notice that they were so prosperous and secure, that they became prolific in producing offspring. They were soon greater in number and wealthier than their hosts, the Egyptians. They were truly in compliance with God's command in Gen. 1:28 – "*Be fruitful, and multiply, and*

Personal Notes

replenish the earth, and subdue it ...." The change came when both Joseph and the Pharaoh familiar with their story died.

Israel continued to multiply and grow in wealth. But over time, the Egyptians became envious and afraid of a people that were becoming greater than they. There eventually arose a Pharaoh who took steps to curb Israel's progress. He subdued them through enslavement, and the unlawful appropriation of their wealth. In an effort to prevent their population from rising any further, he introduced an evil genocidal plan – Hebrew midwives were to kill every newborn male. It is in this atmosphere that Moses is born.

Moses was saved from certain death by the love, faith, ingenuous plan of his mother, and the providence of God. He was adopted into Pharaoh's family as an infant. In an instant he was moved from a hut to a palace – evidence that nothing is impossible with God. This was a master stroke in God's plan for our redemption – He positioned Moses to learn the ways of his enemies. How can we fight the devil if we are unaware of his methods?

The story picks up momentum as we witness Moses' slaying of the Egyptian, and his subsequent flight into the desert to avoid prosecution by the Egyptian authorities. This takes him from the first preparatory phase of his assignment to the second – his Wilderness Experience and encounter with the Living God through his Burning Bush Experience. He grew up with power and authority, accustomed to the obedience of servants. Now he is humbled in the presence of our Creator. This brokenness prepares him as a fit vessel for God's use to deliver his kin from Egyptian slavery.

The Battle is The Lord's

We watch as Moses receives his historical assignment from Jehovah, "*Come now therefore, and I will send thee unto Pharaoh, that thou mayest bring forth my people the children of Israel out of Egypt*" *(Ex. 3:10*). At first the brother makes all sorts of excuses to avoid the task. But deep down inside he knew that his knowledge of Egyptian ways made him the most suitable candidate for the

Personal Notes

position. Further, this was God who was sending him, and not alone – God promised to be with him, backing every move. But I believe that God's most persuasive argument was His working of miracles. He changed Moses' staff to a serpent, and his hand into a leprous member of his body. Both were restored to their original state. We can just imagine what was going through Moses' mind – seeing is believing. His faith grows with every experience.

Four hundred years and three million souls after Israel entered Egypt, God sent a '*deliverer*' to lead them out of slavery. The fugitive Moses boldly enters Pharaoh's court with what must have sounded as the most outrageous demand. Pharaoh was adamant – Israel will remain as slaves. Then the plagues came: the blood all over the land, save Goshen, seven days without drinking water, not to mention the inability to bathe – the place stank. Next were the frogs – frogs in the dough, under the bed, in the bathroom, in clothing, frogs everywhere. But we remain dumb spiritual observers – as incredulous as it may seem, Pharaoh puts off the release of Israel for another day. What's wrong with this guy? So God sent lice. We watch the Egyptians scratch, and their animals become restless. Now here comes the flies, disgusting swarms all over the place. Notwithstanding these plagues, Pharaoh remains resolute. At the height of each incident he agrees to release the people, but reverts to his old stubborn self when each plague is removed. So God steps up the pace.

The wealth of Egypt is now attacked with a progression that leads to Restoration for Israel. All of the cattle and animals owned by the Egyptians were killed, including horses, asses, and camels. Boils and blains followed – this was probably cowpox for the animals, and smallpox for humans. No one could work. The Egyptian economy was in trouble. But would Pharaoh relent – no way. He is so tough, that his judgment was clouded by his desire to defeat God – despite the mounting evidence of the odds against him.

How does Pharaoh view his predicament? His economy is shot. There is no trade. People are afraid to enter Egypt because of the plagues. The Egyptian

Personal Notes

Personal Notes

dollar is devalued, and stocks plummet on the market. Why does he continue to hold Israel, the cause of his woes? I venture to suggest that he is holding unto them for the same reason that we purchase many appliances and other consumer goods from third world countries – cheap labor. The release of Israel would mean hard work for the Egyptians.

The hail and fire which follow, devastate the land further. Crops are destroyed, and those who remained in the field perished. Whatever survived the hail, was completely destroyed by the locusts. Pharaoh repents, but then his numb heart grows cold once more. He even ignores the advice of his ministers who asked him, *"How long shall this man be a snare unto us? Let the men go, that they may serve the Lord their God: knowest thou not yet that Egypt is destroyed?"* (Ex. 10:7). At this point it seems to me that Pharaoh's refusal to release Israel was based on pride – he just did not like to lose. How else can we explain his reluctance in the face of a systematic erosion of his power and wealth? The final two blows overshadowed that pride and any remaining resistance to the will of God.

It is now necessary for the Egyptians to work in order to repair the damage to their personal lives, and to the economy as a whole. But three days of darkness ensued, and prevented any business deals from going through. Everyone had to stay in his place. What made matters worse was the fact that the darkness had no effect on the people of Israel – they had light in Goshen. The grand finale, however, was the destruction of every first born male. Before this event, a curious but significant occurrence draws our attention.

What About The Money?

Remember way back when Israel first came to Egypt, how they were wealthy and then increased tremendously? Remember how they were first enslaved and what happened to that wealth – do you know of a rich slave in slavery? The Egyptians took it all. Well now the scene is about to be changed, as God prepares to deliver Israel from bondage. The just God that we serve will not allow them to leave Egypt without what is rightfully theirs. This includes the interest that would have accrued over the years of their enslavement – imagine, 400 years of interest. God gave Israel favor with the Egyptians whose hearts were now mellow because they witnessed the power of God on behalf of Israel. He directs Israel to demand gold, silver and costly apparel from the Egyptians. Indeed, *"When a man's ways please the Lord, He maketh even his enemies to be at peace with him" (Prov. 16:7).* Israel left Egypt with wealth – "..... *The wealth of the sinner is laid up for the just" (Prov. 13:22).* We notice the ease with which the children of Israel are able to obtain jewelry and other items of financial worth from the Egyptians. This must be God! Now they are prepared to follow Moses without hesitation.

Then, we observe another curious phenomenon. The children of Israel lock themselves indoors following Moses' instructions. They mark their doors with the blood of the lamb as the angel of death moves over the land. It took tremendous faith in God for them to stand dressed and ready to go, without an inkling of where they were going – it's always difficult to leave the familiar for the unknown. But even as they ate the 'Passover' in faith, things began to happen. While the sound of death emanated from the homes of the Egyptians as every first born died, Israel was blessed with a resurgence of life. Old people regained their youthful strength, blind eyes were opened, the lame were healed – a full deliverance by the Lord. The Bible records "*.... And there was not one feeble person among their tribes" (Ps. 105:37).* They were truly prospering and enjoying good health as their souls received the Word of God through Moses (3 John 2).

A Miracle is not Enough

Now comes the true test. Removed from familiar surroundings, fear begins to step in. The devil refuses to give up without a fight. Once more, God demonstrates His faithfulness – He removes the threat of the pursuing Egyptians. They are 'lost at sea' – the Red Sea envelopes them after the children of Israel are firmly on the other bank. Despite this mighty showing by God, Israel soon became discontented because of the hardships of the desert. They asked for food,

Personal Notes

He gave them 'manna.' They asked for meat, He sends them quails. They complained of thirst, He gave them water from a rock. But nothing God did satisfied them. The manna, quails, and water were each a great miracle. Take the manna for example. Each person was entitled to an omer, or 4 pints per day by our standard (Ex. 16:16). Imagine how much manna God supplied daily for three million souls – approximately 1,500,000 gallons per day.

Quails are small birds. It would take tons of bird meat each day to feed such a multitude in the wilderness. What about water coming out of a rock to quench the thirst of three million people? It would take a conservative average of 6 gallons of water per day per person. That is, 18 million gallons of water from the rock each day. This is an awesome God at work – supplying the needs of His people, no matter what the needs were.

Like Israel who ignored or soon forgot these miracles, we allow fear to rob us of our possessions. We wonder whether the God who supplied the manna, quails and water can help us pay the electric or telephone bill. We speculate on His ability to supply all our needs according to his riches in glory by Christ Jesus. Miracles of the past are not enough – including those miracles that occurred in our own lives. My friend *".... Is my hand shortened at all, that it cannot redeem? Or have I no power to deliver? ...." (Isa. 50:2).* We must be confident that what God has promised, He is able also to perform (Rom. 4:21).

The Wrong Direction – God's Wisdom

Our observation of the exodus from Egypt was exhilarating and spiritually refreshing. But wait a minute! We notice that to our left from Goshen, and only a few miles away, is the Great Sea. Following that coastline due North East would lead us into the Promised land – Canaan, a mere 200 miles away by that route. Why then, was God leading Israel due South – a direction that was opposite to their ultimate destination? The answer to this question is found in Ex. 13:17, *"And it came to pass, when Pharaoh had let the people go, that God led them not through the way of the land of the Philistines, although that was near, for God*

Personal Notes

said, Lest peradventure the people repent when they see war, and they return to Egypt."

Personal Notes

Israel was not ready for war after so many years of slavery. God needed to prepare them for the battles ahead. Time was the necessary element to achieve this goal. God's action is justified when, at Kadesh-Barnea, approximately 50 miles away from "Milk and Honey,' they grew fearful because of the report that there were giant warriors in that land. *"And wherefore had the Lord brought us unto this land, to fall by the sword, that our wives and our children should be a prey? Were it not better for us to return into Egypt? And they said one to another, Let us make a captain, and let us return into Egypt" (Num. 14:3, 4).*

God's initial plan seems to be to teach Israel to depend on Him as their sole source. He utilized their wilderness experience during the three months it took them to get to Sinai. At Sinai he instructed them on laws of hygiene and sanitation, establishing the natural means toward their continued good health. Contemporary medical practitioners are amazed at the detailed directions given by God. The bubonic and other plagues which ravished Medieval Europe could have been avoided, or at least brought to an earlier halt, had there been freedom to give the book of Leviticus some attention.

The journey to Sinai covered 225 miles approximately, and took three months. But they remained there for over one year to be schooled in the ways of the lord. When they were physically and spiritually ready for the trials ahead, God allowed them to move the remaining 180 miles to Kadesh-Barnea, the spring board to Canaan. This push took longer than necessary because of Israel's continued rebellion. They questioned God's ability at least ten times during this phase (Num. 14:22). They had now covered 405 miles in about two years. Their destination seemed so near, but their fear and rebellion delayed their entry for another 40 years.

Israel had to take a circuitous route to arrive at Jericho, skirting the border of Edom. Four hundred and fifty miles, and many avoidable battles later, Joshua led them into Canaan. They had traversed about 855 miles to arrive at their destination – a journey that could have been accomplished by covering half that distance, and within God's original plan of two years, instead of forty two.

I believe that there is a lesson for each of us here. Obedience to God's plans and ways of doing things will lead us away from sin (Egypt), and we will be richer for it. Sometimes the shorter way is fraught with danger (land of the Philistines). The longer route allows us to mature, until we become firmly rooted and grounded in the word of God (The wilderness of Sinai and Paran). Adherence to God's commands brings us to a place where we can appropriate the wealth of the 'System' (The land of Canaan). Fear, disobedience, and rebellion will delay or totally prevent us from walking in the promises of God, enjoying the 'Milk and Honey.' The bottom line is that God is the only true source for all our needs, and we should trust Him implicitly.

This episode of the exodus of the children of Israel from Egypt is atypical of the various phases of God's plan of redemption as recorded in the Old Testament. Israel maintained an on-again, off-again relationship with our Creator. When they obeyed Him, they prospered and lived in peace. When they were disobedient, they experienced periods of servitude to other nations.

Another glowing example is represented in the lives of David and his son Solomon. David's obedience to God saw him triumph over all his enemies, gaining wealth without measure in the process. Consequently, Israel was able to enjoy a legacy of fortitude and peace under Solomon. Their wealth was so great, that other nations expressed awe at the grandeur and benevolence of God's favor. In essence, true prosperity was evident in Israel. In common parlance, "they had it made in the shade – they had money to burn!" Their experiences should service as a 'Learning Tree' for each of us today. However, we need to move forward to a point 2000 years beyond. Here we would be able to examine the life of the man Jesus, the perfect example and instructor of financial management – He is the Messiah!

Personal Notes

Jesus – The Only Way

Personal Notes

The world was lost legally to Satan by the disobedience of one man – Adam I. It was therefore necessary for a man to regain it by legal means as well. Jesus, Adam II, was that man. When Jesus asked His mother, *"…. wist ye not that I must be about my Father's business?" (Luke 2:49),* what business was He referring to? It seems to me that Jesus was reminding Mary of the angel's words to Joseph when she was commissioned for the glorious work of being mother to the Messiah – *"He shall save His people from their sins" (Matt. 1:21).* This business of Jesus then, was the redemption of the sinner - it led him to the Court at the Cross.

The second Adam had to be like the first before the 'Fall' in order to present an irrefutable case in Court – He had to be without sin. Jesus was the *'perfect'* man for the job. His birth through the Holy Spirit inaugurated His sinless entry, and His way of life established it. He was perfect for the reception of all our sins, suffering, sickness and disease – Isaiah 53 gives a clear prophetic picture of His accomplishments at the Cross. When Jesus said, *"It is finished,"* (John 19:30), I believe He was referring to the fact that He had succeeded in luring Satan into a successful trap – *"And I, if I be lifted up from the earth, will draw all men unto me" (John 12:32).* It is often said that if Satan knew God's plan, the Cross would have never occurred. It was a mystery to him (1 Cor. 2:7, 8). Jesus' resurrection from the dead was the culmination of the structure for our salvation. The Way was made manifest. Redemption thus became a matter of our response to Jesus' sacrifice at Calvary.

The veil of the temple was torn from top to bottom at the time of Jesus' death. Symbolically, this indicated the demise of tradition, and the freedom for you and me to enter personally into the Holy of Holies. There is now no further need to sacrifice sheep and goats – we were bought with a price – the precious blood of Jesus, the blood that would never lose its power.

Yes, it was finished just over 2000 years ago so that those who believe in the sacrifice Jesus made, and accepted Him as Lord and Savior, could be redeemed. If that's you, then know that you are redeemed from the curse of the law, and have the authority and power to overcome Satan through the very blood Jesus shed, and by the word of your own testimony (Gal. 3:13; Rev.12:11). Our testimony should be that:

> We are victors because Jesus completed the race on our behalf.
>
> We are born again of the incorruptible seed of the word of God that lives and abides forever (1 Pet. 1:23).
>
> We are washed in the blood of the Lamb, all our sins are forgiven (Eph. 1:7).
>
> We are delivered from the power of darkness, we are now members Of the kingdom of God (Col. 1:13).
>
> We are above only, and not beneath (Deut. 28:13).
>
> We are now dead to sin (Rom. 6:2, 11).
>
> We have been reconciled to God – to enjoy the blessing Adam I had before he sinned (2 Cor. 5:18).
>
> We are now joint heirs with Christ (Rom. 8:17).
>
> We have been given power over all the power of the enemy (Luke 10:19).

When Jesus shouted from the Cross, *It is finished,"* the legal battle was over. The devil was defeated. You and I are now free to walk this earth as kings/Queens, and God's priests (Rev. 1:6). The devil is subject to our authority. However, such authority is maintained only if we enforce it with the power released to us by Jesus.

The Court at the Cross was adjourned until that final Day of Judgment, that notable day when Jesus Himself presides, and administers the justice that is inevitable. On that day, the Lake of Fire will become a reality for Satan and those who choose to follow him. I am glad that none of us fall within that category – we are REDEEMED!

Personal Notes

What Has Money Got To Do With It?

Redemption is priceless! That's why sinless Jesus had to pay the price we could not, for a debt He did not owe personally. But the road to Redemption, well, that's a different matter. The Bible is replete with instances of Israel's use of money in the redemptive process.

1. They offered Edom money for the use of water and victuals as they made their way to Canaan. Edom refused their offer, and threatened them instead.
2. God commanded Moses to use money as the means to redeem all the first born of Israel apart from the Levites (5 shekels each). Moses collected a total of 26,065 shekels (Num. 3:46 – 51). Joseph and Mary honored this command when they brought Jesus to the temple on the eight day after His birth – He was their first born, and not of the tribe of Levi (Luke 2:21 – 23).

More recently, we witnessed the fulfillment of prophecy as the State of Israel was reborn in 1948. Then Israel began a program of repatriation to bring Jews 'home' from all over the world. Jews came from China (yes, there are Chinese Jews), from Russia and several other parts of the globe (Isaiah 43: 4-6). But Operation Solomon was the clincher. This was the dramatic airlift of 14,500 Black Ethiopian Jews from Addis Ababa to Israel on May 25, 1991 – an operation that lasted for thirty six hours. It is said that Israel made a secret deal with the communist Ethiopian government in 1985 to ransom the Black Jews. Regardless of whether a ransom was paid or not, the logistic implications and cost to bring Jews from all over the world must have been stupendous. This does not even take into account the cost of housing, clothing, and nutrition – an initial necessity for resettlement. Without money, none of this would have been possible.

A reflection on the Beginning brings to mind God's wisdom and foresight, as he provided all we would need from the inception. Adam I lost it all. God, with grace and mercy, paved the way for us to regain it – Adam II paid the necessary price. Yet today most of it still remains in the wrong hands.

Personal Notes

MANAGING GOD'S FINANCES

Personal Notes

I believe that as we grow to understand the necessary use of money in the redemptive process, more and more Saints will approach the management of God's finances with greater resilience. We will endeavor to remain debt free as God enables us to prosper. In the same manner that Israel adopted and funded the repatriation of Jews, Saints will fund missionaries, outreaches, Christian television programs, and every necessary work that serves to foster the End-Time Harvest of souls. GLORY TO GOD!

MANAGING GOD'S FINANCES

Chapter 3

THE BLOOD OF JESUS – IT'S IMPACT

The preceding chapter highlighted God's plan of redemption which culminated at Calvary. It is imperative that we understand that none of this would have been possible without the willingness of Jesus to be the ultimate sacrifice. But there is one single factor which is sung about and given great attention in Christian circles – the blood of Jesus. Do we really understand the importance of His shed blood? Do we truly recognize the impact of His blood in the process of reconciliation to God? His blood was the vehicle through which the legal and Divine Transaction was completed. It seems therefore, that in order to understand why we need to manage God's finances, we need to understand what was achieved through His blood.

We as Christians usually focus on Isaiah 53: 4, 5 or 1 Peter 2:24 to reflect on the impact of Jesus' blood in our lives. However, we seldom recognize that His blood was actually shed in seven different places, and that there is an actual relationship between those occasions and our redemption. In an effort to understand this transaction, we need to examine God's instructions to the priests in regards to the annual cleansing of the people of Israel. Let us journey once more to the Biblical times of the Old Testament.

The Blood of Bulls and Goats

The Old Testament contains many events and rituals that offer symbolic references to experiences in the New Testament. I believe that none is as poignant as those events depicting the various blood sacrifices commanded by God. For example, in the book of Exodus 12, especially verse 7, we read of the Passover Lamb. The Israelites were to ensure that no bone was broken, and that the blood of this lamb was placed on the door of each home in a manner that we now know represented the Cross. It is significant that none of Jesus' bones was broken while He hung on the Cross.

Personal Notes

Personal Notes

However, the ritual that offers the greatest symbolism to Jesus' shed blood, and our redemption, can be found in Leviticus 16 - emphasis on verses 14, 18 and19. One of the observations that are usually overlooked is the examination of the animals to be offered – they were examined for four days to ensure that they were without blemish. Similarly, Jesus, after entering Jerusalem during that faithful week, was examined by the Pharisees, Sadducees, scribes and lawyer, for four days before Pilate announced "*I find no fault in this man …*" (Luke 23: 14, 15). Further, we see that one aspect of the ritual was to sprinkle the blood of the sin offering seven times on the altar, and on the Mercy Seat. In like manner, Jesus shed His blood in seven different places, and each occasion served to eliminate some obstacle that was introduced through Adam's sin. It was no longer necessary to depend on the blood of bullocks and goats – Jesus was the ultimate sacrificial Lamb. The following discussion will identify each area in which Jesus shed His blood, and the redemptive work accomplished as a result.

The Garden of Gethsemane

Dr. Luke recorded the episode of Gethsemane in chapter 22 and verse 44 of the Gospel named after him. He observed that Jesus was in such agony when He prayed, that drops of blood flowed from His head. This is known in medical circles as *hematidrosis* – a condition that occurs when an individual resists the body's attempt to 'shut down' during a period of severe stress. This resistance causes the blood cells to rupture, and the blood to mingle with the sweat glands, eventually exiting through the pores of the skin. But what is so significant about this incident in Gethsemane? The answer lies in another garden – the Garden of Eden.

The first act of sin on earth was in disobedience to God. It's as if Adam was saying, "God, I know what you said, and I know what your will is concerning this matter of eating from the Tree of the Knowledge of Good and Evil. But you gave me the ability to make a choice, and this is my decision – not your will but mine be done." In essence, Adam transferred his allegiance to Satan, who, for all intent and purposes now controlled his will.

Personal Notes

Jesus' first act towards redemption was to regain our will power and authority. He shed His blood in Gethsemane while uttering the words, *"Father, if thou be willing, remove this cup from me: nevertheless not my will, but thine be done" (Luke 22:42).* This act of loyalty coupled with the ratification by His blood, served to nullify Adam's treason, and to restore our will power to our individual control. The Roman Praetorium was the next site for the progressive and legal steps toward our deliverance and reconciliation to God.

In The Praetorium

Two distinct and independent blood transactions occurred when Jesus was brought before Pontius Pilate in the Roman Praetorium – He was scourged (tortured, whipped), and a crown of thorns was placed on His head (John 19: 1-5; Matt. 27:29). Thirty nine stripes were administered during the scourging at the whipping post. It is said that there are thirty nine different categories of diseases in the world. We can therefore conclude that Jesus, through His blood paid the covenantal price to free us from all diseases which were heralded in through sin (1 Peter 2:24).

When the soldiers placed the crown of ***thorns*** on His head, they actually helped to destroy the curse in Gen. 3:17, 18. The ground (not Adam) was cursed so that it would be difficult to manage, bringing forth ***thorns*** and thistles. This relates to a negative economic situation. Our economic viability was restored when Jesus bled through the thorns on His head.

The fourth and fifth occasions are related – His pierced hands and feet while on the Cross (Ps. 22:16-18). The blood shed through these parts of His body was meant to restore the authority and dominion originally given to Adam in Genesis 1: 26-28.

Many theologians believe that the real cause of Jesus' death was a broken heart – both literally and figuratively. When His side was pierced by the Roman soldier, a mixture of water and blood flowed from the wound. This was an indication that the pericardium was punctured, releasing the serous fluid which served to keep the heart buoyant and protected. But His heart was already ruptured, hence the

Personal Notes

mixture of blood with the serum. According to Luke 4: 18, a part of Jesus' assignment was to heal the broken hearted. His heart was broken so that ours could be healed. All of our broken dreams and aspirations were addressed and restored through this one act.

The final place was necessary because of God's declaration to Satan in Gen. 3: 15 – the seed of the woman would bruise his head, and he, Satan would bruise the heel of her seed. This is perhaps the most difficult aspect of the Divine transaction to understand, that is, until we perceive that the statement embodied some figurative implications. Remember Achilles from Greek mythology? He could only be harmed through his heel. The heel represents a place of vulnerability. Jesus was 'vulnerable' because of His love for others – He gave His life for us. He was emotionally troubled when He was rejected – He wept for Jerusalem. The persecution of the Jews, and the betrayal by one of His own disciples, all had a toll on His emotions and on His heart. That's why it's believed that He died as a result of the emotional damage to His heart – His heel was bruised.

The good news is that because of his obedience, even unto the Cross, we are redeemed. But there were still two further acts to complete our reconciliation to God – he had to bruise Satan's head, and then to ratify the Messianic covenant in the heavenly tabernacle. After His death, Jesus wrested the key of death and Hell from the devil (Rev. 1:18). That must have really surprised Satan as he attempted to retain possession of all that pertained to life. He ended up with a bruised head. The final vestige of power on earth was restored to the right hands. Then, just as we read in Leviticus 16 about the final act of pouring the remainder of the blood around the altar, Jesus did the same with His at the Heavenly Altar (Heb. 9:1 – 15). This final act paved the way for the reconciliation of all those who believe in Him.

What does this all mean to you and me? If we are redeemed, it means that we were bought back, restored to our former state. If we are reconciled to God, that means we can walk with Him in the cool of the day just as Adam did before sin (2 Cor. 5:17-21). But with this new privilege comes the same responsibility that Adam had – the need for obedience to God's will and His way. In the same way that His will was for Adam to be a loyal and efficient steward of the Garden of Eden, in like manner we are to be excellent stewards at managing His finances. Why finances? Because it's the medium through which His covenants with humankind will be established (Deut. 8:18) and afford others the opportunity to enjoy the same benefits we now do. We, as born again Christians, live under the Edenic Blessing. But do you truly understand what it represents, especially as it relates to managing God's economy? A study of His essential covenants should provide us with the answers

Personal Notes

Chapter 4

THE MAIN COVENANTS IN GOD'S PLAN OF REDEMPTION

Personal Notes

The Bible is replete with various promises made both by God and His people. The former maintains His position with integrity, while the latter often renege on their commitment. As Christians we recognize that the covenants made by God are unique and without flaw. What we also need to realize is that there is an eternal purpose to those introduced by God – they were all geared to facilitate our redemption. It would therefore serve our purpose to examine the essential covenants that affect our lives one way or another. In order to obtain a firm grasp of the rudiments involved, we will explore the background and ritualistic implications of the essential covenants.

In the book of Genesis, chapters 1 through 3, we read about creation. The gospel according to John chapter 1 indicates that everything was created by God – without Him, nothing was created. This suggests that all systems in existence proceeded from God – including covenants. But what does a covenant really represent? My understanding is that a covenant is a unique promise between two or more intelligent parties of consenting age. It is legally binding at most times, but morally binding at all times. It is mutually beneficial to both parties at most times, but can also stem from the generosity of one party with power to another without – *Hesed.*

Kevin Conner and Ken Malmin in their book *The Covenant,* explain that the word covenant in Scripture refers to an agreement or a contract between men, or between God and man. Contemporary methods of establishing a covenant can range from the signing of a legal document such as the marital agreement, to the shaking of hands. In ancient times, the preferred way necessitated the shedding of blood, and was termed *'Cutting Covenant.'* Regardless of the form it took, the underlying factor was the faith demonstrated by participants who were assured that the promises would be maintained. The writer of the Book of Romans, chapter 4, points out in verse 21 that Abraham was fully persuaded that what God had promised, He was also capable of performing. Why was Abraham so convinced of God's ability and loyalty? The answer could be found in Genesis 15:8-10, 17, and 18. God made a blood covenant with Abraham whose only responsibility was to be obedient in following God's directions. Abraham's trust was based on his own experience of covenants, and the implications for those involved. A description of the ancient ritual should assist in granting us an empathetic understanding of Abraham's position.

Personal Notes

The Ancient Covenant Ritual

The covenants of old were introduced to bring a balance between the *strengths* and *weaknesses* of the people. For example, in the agrarian society of the time, a farmer, skilled in agriculture, was likely to be unskilled in warfare. Yet, he needed to safeguard his crop from marauders. Toward that end, he and his family would enter an agreement with those who were skilled in warfare – the intent being to obtain protection for the harvest. Such an agreement would be mutually beneficial, since the warrior would protect the farmer's crop, and in return receive his sustenance from the very items he served to protect. This custom was prevalent, and obviously demanded complete loyalty and commitment – death being the penalty for noncompliance. There was therefore an intense discussion before such an agreement was adopted. In recognition of the binding nature of these agreements, an official ceremony was held with relevant rituals which depicted the serious implications of the contract.

The ritualistic process was clearly defined in most ancient communities. It followed a formal pattern that left no doubt concerning the intent and legal authority of the parties involved to engage the covenant. The following sequence of events outlines a progression that culminated with a bond between the contracting individuals or families:

1. An appropriate representative was chosen from each family.

Personal Notes

2. Preparation was made for the ceremony – choosing a proper site, and animal/s without blemish. Then the actual ceremony would begin.

Choosing The Family Representative

Each family had to choose a representative that identified with the strength of that family. For example the warrior family would present their best fighter, while the farmers would send their best farmer. These two individuals would be given the honor of *'Cutting Covenant,'* on behalf of their respective families.

Preparation for The Ceremony

It is imperative that the parties agree on an appropriate site. This is necessary in order to enable every family member to have a vantage point from which to observe the ceremony. It is not simply a matter of viewing the process, but rather has legal implications which identify each member as a witness, and therefore bound individually to the agreement.

The final preparation is perhaps the most important prior to the actual ceremony – choosing the covenant animal. This animal must be without blemish. It is killed at the chosen site, and cut down the middle so that each half lies opposite the other, with a clear passage between them. The blood is allowed to flow into the passage. The formal ceremony commences after these preparations.

The Covenant Ceremony.

The two families now gather at the site, standing at opposite ends of the slain animal .The chosen representatives each stand at opposite ends of the passage between the sacrificial animal. The following ritual ensues:

a. First, they exchange coats. This signifies, ***"Who I am, and all that I am, I give myself to you"*** - authority to take action in each other's affairs.

They next exchange the tools of their respective trades. The warrior receives a farm tool, while the farmer receives a weapon of warfare. This indicates that, ***"I give you my strength. Your enemies are mine. I stand with you unto death."***

b. They then walk toward each other in the blood, passing each other twice. They stop in the center to announce, ***"Even as this animal has died, I stand with you in the midst of death. Standing in the blood, I make promises I can never break."***

c. The promises are then repeated by each individual – the blessings of the covenant. God is made the third party and witness to the covenant as each individual swears by God to keep the promises.

d. Each of the two individuals then cuts either his wrist or hand. This signifies that the life blood of his family was being shed. Next, an oath to keep the covenant is uttered while the hand is held high so that the blood flows down the arm. It ends with the plea, ***"So help me God!"*** The scar which will never go away represents a sign that the families are now one.

e. The perpetual testimony of the covenant is the name change. They add the surname of the other family to theirs. This act is similar to the adoption of a hyphenated name by some married individuals. For example, if the farmer's surname was Potato and the warrior's Shield, then the farmer's surname would now become Potato-Shield, and the warrior's Shield-Potato. This is a signal of strength to all other families.

Personal Notes

Personal Notes

The final ritual is the covenant meal. The appointed leaders share a cup of wine and state, ***"Drink my life's blood as I drink your life's blood. I see you fulfilling all the terms of the covenant as I fulfill your life."*** They also share a piece of bread with a final statement; ***Take me – all that I am. Eat of me, I am yours."***[3] This concludes the ceremony. Now we can understand why Abraham was fully persuaded that what God had promised, He was also able to perform (Rom. 4:21). With this background, we can now examine the essential covenants that have a bearing on our redemption. We are better positioned to understand why our salvation is assured by the blood of Jesus – we can understand the process He went through as the sacrificial Lamb.

The Essential Covenants

The authors of "The Covenant," Kevin Conner and Ken Malmin, identified nine main covenants that impacted Israel, and which continue to affect us to this day. There are obviously other covenants that were enacted during Israel's long history, but nine were considered major because they each fitted directly into God's plan for redemption and reconciliation. The following is a description of each of these nine contracts. I have taken the liberty to adjust two names and the sequence based on my understanding of their individual importance.

1). The Eternal Covenant (also known as The Everlasting Covenant)

This covenant embodies God's eternal plan. It was made in eternity, where there is no time. Yet, time must have been a consideration since the plan included God's creation and the earthly manifestation of a chronological system – encompassing from creation to redemption. This covenant therefore included the fullness of the Godhead, and made provision for all other covenants to follow. We humans were excluded from the execution of this covenant – only the Father, Son, and the Holy Spirit took active roles in its enactment. However, we were affected by its provision.

In this covenant, the Father serves as the one who gives the words of promise. The Son has a unique role as both the offerer and offering – the one who offers the sacrifice, while being the sacrifice Himself. The Holy Spirit is the seal, and the one who actually executes the covenant. Note Eph. 1:9-11; Heb. 13:20; Rom. 8:27-30; and Eph.3:11. The second covenant was made with Adam before sin, while the remaining seven were introduced at various times in our progression toward redemption and reconciliation.

2). The Edenic Covenant.

This agreement was made between God and mankind before sin. It was special in that sense. Nevertheless, it contained all the elements required for the ratification of a covenant:

a. ***The Words*** – Gen. 1:28, 29; 2:5, 15, 17. As with all blood covenants, these words include both blessings and curses.

b. ***The blood of The Covenant*** – Gen. 2:18-25. Adam's sinless blood was shed in the first recorded surgery – removing one of his ribs to fashion Eve.

c. ***The Seal*** – Gen. 2:17; 3:22-24. Prior to sin, Adam was free to eat from the Tree of Life. That was the seal. Sin caused that privilege to be rescinded, and the eternal seal was withheld.

3). The Adamic Covenant

This was the beginning of the redemptive covenants. Although Adam deserved both physical and spiritual death for his treason, God exercised mercy and compassion. This was all in the eternal plan, and had its foundation in the Edenic covenant mentioned above. Gen. 3:14-19 gives an insight into God's action of love for His creation despite the disobedience.

4). The Noahic Covenant

This covenant is explained throughout the pages of Gen. chapters 6 to 9. After the 'Fall' of mankind in the Garden of Eden, the Adamic covenant was ignored by the people, and sin became rampant. However, one man, Noah, found favor with God because of his exceptional devotion to his Creator – he observed the covenant. Noah and his family were therefore separated from God's judgment on the wicked which resulted in the Flood. A new covenant was made with Noah

Personal Notes

– man was given an opportunity for a fresh start. This new covenant was similar to the Edenic covenant, and included all of God's creation. God was paving the way for our redemption.

Personal Notes

5). The Abrahamic Covenant.

This covenant, above all others in the Old Testament, offers the most comprehensive insight to God's eternal plan. It isolates the human vehicle chosen directly to guide us by faith to redemption, and demonstrates God's ingenious methodology to effect reconciliation with His creation. Abraham was the willing seed through whom the nation of Israel was birthed. However, it is imperative to recognize that from the inception, God indicated to him that he would be the instrument through which all other nations would be blessed (Gen. 12:1-3). This covenant is the basis of our relationship with Christ. It includes prior and subsequent covenants which all lead toward the redemption of mankind. A biblical perspective of this truth is found when Gen. 11:10-32 is read in conjunction with Gen. 12:1-3, and Gen. 15:1-21.

6). The Mosaic Covenant.

This covenant concerns Israel only. It came 430 years after the Abrahamic Covenant. It was not meant to be a replacement, but was rather introduced as a segment in fulfillment of the former. It is appropriately referred to as the "Law Covenant" because God used it to illustrate His standards for righteous living – standards by which all mankind should be guided. Consequently, this covenant was very explicit, and can be considered the most complete expression of a covenant in all Scripture. Israel was the chosen model to impact the rest of the world through obedience to this covenant. The ratification of this covenant was reproduced in Ex. 24:1- 8 (note in particular verses 7 and 8); Deut. 5:1-5.

7). The Palestinian Covenant.

God introduced this covenant when Israel was ready to possess their inheritance – it was all about land. It was given to the second generation of Israel in the wilderness. This covenant reflected both the Abrahamic and Mosaic covenants – the former promised the land, the latter confirmed it, while the

Personal Notes

Palestinian Covenant made occupation of the land conditional. The first generation out of Egypt received the Mosaic Covenant at Mt. Sinai, while the second generation received the Palestinian Covenant in the plains of Moab. The entire chapter of Deut. 28 and 29:1 give instructions concerning this covenant.

8). The Davidic Covenant.

We who believe in Christ, and are therefore redeemed, are kings and priests to God. The Davidic Covenant is all about this kingship – he was chosen by God. This covenant can be traced back to the Edenic covenant, and forward to the Messianic covenant which fulfills all nine essential covenants under review. This covenant was made with David after Saul's death, and demonstrated God's faithfulness to his seed, his house, his throne, and his kingdom – both naturally, and spiritually. Information to this effect can be found in 2 Sam. 7:10-16.

9). The Messianic Covenant (New Covenant).

Once again the information supplied by Conner and Malmin presents a succinct but powerful description of God's intention through His covenants. This time, in pointing to what I consider the main covenant, these able researchers wrote that, *"The New Covenant was made by the Lord Jesus Christ immediately prior to His death at Jerusalem. It was made with the twelve apostles, who represented the House of Israel and the House of Judah, after the flesh, but were the foundation of the New Covenant Church, being the twelve apostles of the Lamb. It became the fulfillment of all previous Covenants, fulfilling and abolishing in itself their temporal elements and making possible their everlasting elements. The New Covenant makes possible and brings the believer into the Everlasting Covenant, thus completing the cycle of Covenantal revelation."*[4]

It should be noted that whereas the other blood covenants required the sacrifice of an animal to satisfy the ritual, the sacrifice here was unique. The Father gave the Son, Jesus, the words of the Covenant. The Son then represented and became the Body and Blood sacrifice of the Covenant, with the Holy Spirit functioning as the Seal. This Covenant made it possible for us to be linked once more with the Eternal Covenant – a complete cycle. We should pay attention to all the words spoken by Jesus during His sojourn on this earth – they each in some way have a bearing on the Messianic Covenant. However, John 12:44-50 and Rom. 9:1 - 5, help us to make the connection. We are assured of the outcome to every covenant. God Himself, the One who cannot lie, has given us His Word – *"My covenant will I not break, nor alter the thing that is gone out of my lips" (Ps. 89:34).*

Personal Notes

Conclusion

In summary, it can be seen that the covenants all implicitly convey a relationship with economic issues. The regular blood covenants engaged among the people of ancient times were adopted for their mutual benefit and survival. The covenants introduced by God were strategically implemented to restore a relationship with Him after the Fall. His promises to Abraham, and consequently to the rest of humanity, clearly identify prosperity as a concomitant aspect of covenantal blessings. God obviously wanted us to enjoy our existence on earth, and knew as well that each of us would need to be viable economically to do so. But more importantly, our individual economic position would be a key factor in our ability to participate meaningfully in His covenants of redemption. Perhaps that's why Jesus spoke so much about money in the Gospels. The next chapter will focus on this statement as we seek further clarity on why we need to manage God's finances.

MANAGING GOD'S FINANCES

Chapter 5

JESUS AND MONEY

Main Text: Matthew 6:24

Was Jesus Wealthy?

There is no scriptural evidence indicating emphatically that Jesus was a wealthy man financially. However, there is no evidence to the contrary either! What we do know is that He was a carpenter by trade (Mk.6:3). It is reasonable to assume that prior to His heavy itinerant schedule during His ministry years, that He earned a living through this trade. Events in His life suggest that He was one of the greatest givers who ever lived – exercising the tenets of true prosperity. How could he accomplish such benevolence without the necessary means? His ministry surely needed funding. Where did the money come from?

Very little is known about Joseph, Mary's husband. We do know that he was also a carpenter (Matt. 13:55). It is very likely that he taught Jesus this skill. But nothing is said of Joseph in Jesus' adult life. Perhaps he died, or left the family for other reasons. Jewish tradition dictated that the first born son should take up the mantle, and become responsible for the family in the absence of the father. Jesus then, must have taken care of His mother and siblings – He had the means to earn a living.

We know that Jesus acknowledged the need for money in His operations. He allowed others to support His ventures to the extent that he needed to appoint a treasurer – Judas (Matt. 27:55, 57; John 13:29). He often bought victuals while on the 'road.' At the feeding of the 5000, as reported in Mark 6:37, His disciples initially thought that He was about to send them to buy bread in the nearby villages. It is evident that Jesus had a successful ministry. Many of His disciples, including the twelve and others, were men and women of worth. Jesus led a comfortable existence, receiving the financial support necessary to complete His agenda.

Personal Notes

His Personal Worth

God did not neglect Jesus in the financial department. Our Heavenly Father ensured that we should see the rewards for obedience through His benevolence to Jesus. We normally look to Jesus as an example of how to live prayerfully and in faith. However, we seldom recognize that His own benevolence to others activated the 'Law of Reciprocity.' But there is also reason to believe that Jesus was blessed from birth. For example:

1. The 'Wise Men' opened His bank account with gold and precious ointments. The Bible records that they knew they were going to worship a King. It is therefore reasonable to believe that they took gifts worthy of a King. Jesus' earthly life commenced with a very strong financial foundation.
2. His parents were not poor. They had their own means of transportation, a donkey. They were capable of paying taxes, and they had money to pay for a place in the inn, had it been available.
3. Jesus himself paid His bills promptly – note His instructions to Peter .to render unto Caesar the things that are Caesar's and unto God the things that pertain to God.
4. He wore expensive clothing – the soldiers cast lots for His expensive seamless coat (John 19:23, 24).
5. His statement to the disciples that they will always have the poor with them, but that He would not always be with them, in itself suggests that He was not poor (Matt. 26:11).
6. Finally, His ministry had need for a treasurer, an indication that there was great financial activity.

Contrary to popular belief, Jesus did experience quality in His financial existence. The legacy He left us, however, was His ability to remain humble, while exercising prudence in all His monetary affairs.

Personal Notes

Jesus' Kingdom Approach to Money Matters

Personal Notes

When we consider Jesus' attitude toward money, we are reminded of that episode next to the treasury in front of the temple. In Mark 12:41-44, we read, *"And Jesus sat over against the treasury, and beheld how the people cast money into the treasury: and many that were rich cast in much. And there came a certain poor widow, and she threw in two mites, which make a farthing. And He called unto Him His disciples, and said unto them, 'Verily I say unto you, that this poor widow hath cast more in, than all they which have cast into the treasury. For all they did cast in of their abundance, but she of her want did cast in all that she had, even all her living.'"*

The spiritual value of money is relative to the condition of one's heart. Show me where your treasure is, and I will show you where your heart is. A penny in the hands of a man whose heart is right before God, is more precious than a thousand dollars in the hands of an unrighteous man. *"No man can serve two masters: for either he will hate the one, and love the other, or else he will hold on to the one, and despise the other. Ye cannot serve God and mammon" (Matt. 6:24).* I once heard someone say that 'wealth in the hands of a righteous man, is souls in the Kingdom of God.'

Money is not to be reverenced as we would a god, but rather to be used to meet our own needs, and then the needs of others with the surplus. It was difficult for the rich young ruler who approached Jesus to understand this concept. The Bible tells us that he went away in sorrow because Jesus wanted him to give away his wealth before joining the ministry. The young man was unaware, and could not conceive that he would have become richer had he obeyed (Matt. 19:21-24). It is only when we embrace a 'Jesus Perspective' of money that we are able to tap into all the benefits of the 'Law of Reciprocity.'

Jesus demonstrated that spending money is not always the best avenue to attain our goals. He had enough in the treasury to buy bread for the 5000 (Mark 6:36-44). Yet, He chose to use what was at hand – five loaves of bread and two fishes. Note that the disciples were not concerned about the cost to feed the multitude, but rather with the availability of such a large quantity of bread that would satisfy the needs of such a crowd. I can just hear them saying "How are we going to carry all this bread?" In one stroke of genius, Jesus nullified this logistical problem, while at the same time saving the expenditure of church funds. There was no need to cart around a huge quantity of bread and fish, instead, the food multiplied as it was distributed. What a miracle!

Sometimes we need to dissuade our children from the penchant to eat out, especially 'fast foods.' We should rather encourage the use of 'what is in the house.' We may save a bundle this way, while redirecting the value of the fast food expenditure to other profitable uses.

In summary, Jesus was a wise steward who understood the true purposes of money, and acted accordingly. He imparted this knowledge to His disciples, and had the information documented for our edification. Money is to be used first to satisfy our own personal needs, following this, we should consider utilizing any surplus to meet the needs of others. It is our heritage as children of God to enjoy the comforts of His Kingdom. Jesus set the example. What we do in our own situations is at the heart of these writings. Let us now look to the apostles for further instructions.

Personal Notes

MANAGING GOD'S FINANCES

Chapter 6

THE APOSTLES AND MONEY

The Misconceptions.

The devil has succeeded in many circles with the lie that to be poor is godly. Many people, saints included, still believe that Jesus and His disciples lived a frugal and poverty centered existence. This is as far from the truth, as the north is from the south.

We have already seen Jesus' approach toward money. He taught His disciples well. They were not poor, but rather knew the true purposes of money. Let us examine a few details of their lives.

The Disciples were Businessmen.

Before Peter, Andrew, James and John met Jesus, they had their own Fishing Enterprise. The scriptures tell us in Mark 1:20 that James and John were the sons of Zebedee, and that they had servants – Peter and Andrew were their partners (Luke 5:10). We also know that they did not sell that business to follow Jesus, but left it for a season. They returned to their vocation temporarily after Jesus was crucified (John 21:3).

Saints, I suggest to you that the disciples were wealthy. It is inconceivable that Jesus would invite them to follow Him at the expense of the good and welfare of their wives and children. Since they had servants, it is likely that they entrusted the business to capable hands under Zebedee's supervision. In other words, their families were provided for as these noble men gave their lives to Jesus and His cause. Jesus ensured they were adequately compensated during their sojourn on earth. According to Mark 10:29, 30, Jesus reinforced His promise to them by declaring, *"Verily, I say unto you, there is no man that hath left house, or brethren, or sisters, or father, or mother, or wife, or children, or lands, for my sake and the gospel's, but he shall receive an hundredfold* ***<u>now in this time</u>****, houses, and brethren, and sisters, and mothers, and children and lands, with persecutions; and in the world to come eternal life."* I believe Jesus was actually

Personal Notes

addressing their itinerant lifestyle which would yield followers wherever they went – people who would be willing to share their wealth and hospitality with the disciples because of the gospel.

Apart from Andrew, Peter, James and John, little is known about the other apostles who were from the original twelve. But Matthew was a Publican (Tax Collector). He must have been a prominent figure in order to secure his own 'Wall Street' area. However, there is evidence that some of the later apostles had wealth. For example:

1. Barnabas owned land. He sold some of it to help others in need (Acts 4:36, 37).
2. Paul's parents were wealthy enough to send him to Jerusalem to study under the renowned scholar Dr. Gamaliel. He himself was a tent maker, a lucrative endeavor because of the great need for tents during that period.

Their love for Jesus was the motivating factor that led them to relinquish all and to follow Him. They transferred their focus from making money to giving it away when appropriate.

Jesus Taught Them How.

I believe that when Jesus sent His disciples out on their own to minister, he purposely sent them without any means of personal financial support. This, to my mind, was to enable them to experience Kingdom principles at work. There are things that money cannot buy – salvation, healing, and deliverance, to name a few (Mark 6:7, 8). The incident with the lame man at the gate 'Beautiful,' illustrates this truth. It was not silver or gold that provided his healing, but rather the power of the Holy Ghost working with his faith and the disciples' (Acts 3:2-8).

The apostles learned the true value of money through the many teachings they received from Jesus. They therefore knew that it could also be used with evil intentions. According to Acts 8:20, 21, Simon the sorcerer offered the apostles money with the hope of receiving power to transfer the anointing of the Holy

Personal Notes

Personal Notes

Ghost by the laying on of hands. Peter's response clearly suggests that the wrong use of money could have severe repercussions. The sorcerer was told, *".... Thy money perish with thee, because thou hast thought that the gift of God may be purchased with money. Thou hast neither part nor lot in this matter: for thy heart is not right in the sight of God."* The apostles were careful to avoid the lure and contamination of evil gains. Nevertheless, like Jesus, they allowed others to contribute to their ministry. In Philippians 4:15-19, we learn that the saints at Philippi sent their financial support often to help Paul's ministry. Jesus taught them well.

Communal Living.

The early Church practiced a lifestyle that we would do well to emulate today. We need renewed minds concerning our relationship with money. We learn in Acts 4 that they had all things common. Some saints went to the extreme of selling their possessions so that the proceeds could be used for the benefit of others – an attempt to ensure that there was an equitable distribution of the necessities of life. No one thought that what he had was all his own. The true meaning of prosperity was in evidence, *"let him that stole steal no more: but rather let him labor, working with his hands the thing which is good, that he may have to give to him that needeth" (Eph. 4:28).* The early church functioned like the Cell Church should be operating today – in self-sufficiency. Only then can we be lenders and not borrowers.

A Dream.

I can just envision a Supermarket and Bank owned and operated by Believers – everything being done in order and in decency. The produce is fresh and neatly packed. All packages carry a Bible verse. Churches from all over purchase goods at an excellent and fair price. The unsaved flock the supermarket to take advantage of the superb bargains and service (really a net to catch the fish). Coupons carry Bible verses which speak of salvation – discounts are obtained when the Bible verses are recited to the cashier. All proceeds from the supermarket are banked in the 'Believers' Restoration Bank Inc.' Believers with accounts in this bank can obtain loans without interest. A fair interest rate is charged to all others (Deut. 23:19, 20). Can you see the results of such an enterprise? Glory To God!

Both Jesus and the apostles established firm guidelines for dealing with money. They were not poor, but great givers – utilizing money for the enhancement of the Kingdom, rather than for personal aggrandizement. We the members of today's Church need to reflect on the apostles' proven financial approaches and methods. We need to acknowledge that money is a good thing when in the hands of a righteous man. Clearly, our prosperity depends on this understanding. We need to be weary of the subtle deceptions which tend to derail sound financial management, and hence the appropriate response through God's benevolence.

Personal Notes

MANAGING GOD'S FINANCES

Chapter 7

DECEPTION IN THE CHURCH – IS MONEY A GODLY INSTRUMENT?

Exposing The Deceiver.

In the beginning Adam was alone with God. There was no question concerning God's voice, Adam knew it well. Then Satan introduced himself, and the confusion began. The Bible tells us that he sometimes appears as the 'angel of light,' (2 cor. 11:14) and that he goes about like a roaring lion seeking whom he may devour (1 Peter 5:8). So men have found it necessary to question themselves – 'Is it my own voice I hear, or is it God's, or worse, is it the devil attempting to lure me into one of his cunning traps?'

A look at some key scriptures should aid us in exposing the true deceiver – Satan. Revelation 12:9, 17 informs us that the devil, also known as Satan, or as that old serpent that deceives the world, was cast out of heaven with a third of the angels because they followed him in his rebellion against God. He has since declared war on all believers. John 8:44 identifies him as a liar, and indeed the father of all lies. According to John 10:10, whereas Jesus came to give life more abundantly, Satan came to kill, steal, and to destroy. He recognizes the power of money in the hands of a righteous man. All his efforts are therefore directed at infiltrating the hearts of unlearned and gullible saints with misconceptions and lies about the use of money.

Is Money A Godly Instrument?

Money in the form of coins is comprised of metal, and in the case of notes, paper and ink – all are inanimate, and without life. However, money serves as a medium of convenient exchange, and therefore people use it. How it is used is the key factor. In the hands of an evil man, it can be used to accomplish despicable things. But in the hands of a righteous man, his paramount objective is to use it for the glory of God. Once we adhere to the Kingdom guidelines for the use of money, we recognize that money in itself is simply a means toward an end.

Personal Notes

MANAGING GOD'S FINANCES

Personal notes

In some church circles it is still believed that money is the root of all evil, and so the accumulation of wealth is seen as sinful. However, the scripture, 1 Tim. 6:10 is seriously misquoted. The scripture actually alerts us to the fact that it's the ***love*** of money (greed) and not money itself that is the root of all evil. God went to great lengths to establish that He desires us to enjoy good living. He created wealth from the inception of His creation. Abraham and all his offspring enjoyed wealth. David, a man after God's own heart was wealthy. Why would God bless each of these men with great wealth if it was sinful?

The truth is that your use of money serves to identify you for the person you truly are. The integrity or flaws of your character are exposed through your use of this instrument. Money corrupts no one. What you do with money is what you already had in your heart. If you are an alcoholic and receive more money, guess what, you will buy more alcohol. A thief who gets away with it, will continue to steal. A drug addict will buy more drugs. But a righteous man will use it to further the things of God. An unknown philosopher once wrote, *'Watch your thoughts, for they become words. Choose your words, for they become actions. Understand your actions, for they become habits. Study your habits, for they will become your character. Develop your character, for it becomes your destiny."* No wonder Satan is determined to keep wealth out of the hands of the saints. If money really corrupted us, the devil would have ensured that we got large sums of it easily; - his ultimate goal is to destroy us.

Look at where most of the money can be found currently – in the hands of the unsaved. The world has made money their god. They have gone after money with greed and lust – similar to Israel's worship of the golden calf in the wilderness. But that road leads to destruction, and that wealth will soon be transferred into the hands of just men who serve God. The recent exposure of issues of greed and corruption, and the many lives that were impacted, indeed the effect on the entire world, demonstrate the truth of God's word (Prov. 13:22). We must remember that although we are in the world, we are not of the world. We have been delivered from the power of darkness, and translated into God's

Kingdom through our belief in Jesus (Col. 1:13). Our principles relative to the use of money should therefore be based on God's system of doing things. I believe that as we continue to position ourselves through obedience to God's ways, we will experience His supernatural intervention in our financial affairs.

In conclusion, let me reaffirm that money, an inanimate instrument in our hands, is not Godly in itself. However, it can be utilized to accomplish Godly tasks. Consequently, it is Godly to desire money for our own needs and to help others. Thank God that more and more Believers are recognizing the deception about money. Saints are responding to God's call on their lives as they understand the true purpose of prosperity. Our task is a futile one without money. More and more saints are becoming entrepreneurs, while others are enhancing their education to enable advancement in the corporate world. Once more, we are on the road to prosperity for our benefit, and for the glory of God. We are no longer deceived. With this revelation comes the responsibility to be good stewards of God's finances. Toward that end it would be appropriate to engage a study of the banking system, and how to use it for the advancement of God's Kingdom.

Personal Notes

MANAGING GOD'S FINANCES

Chapter 8

A HISTORY OF BANKING IN THE USA

Introduction

Personal Notes

One of the main reasons for banking is to facilitate the smooth exchange of money between parties. Banking as we know it is of recent origin (17th century). However, banking existed in ancient times, albeit in a primitive form. Many aspects of modern banking existed then – including foreign exchange, loans, and savings to name a few. But Jews were forbidden from lending to each other with interest (usury, Ex.22:25). They were however permitted to lend to gentiles at a profit (Deut. 23:20).

We need to understand the various facets of banking if we are to appreciate how this institution is being used by Satan to keep us in financial bondage. We need to understand how this system, which in itself is good, can be used for evil purposes. Although this subject seems to be secular in nature, God Himself acknowledged the function of banking. For example, in Matt. 25:27, Jesus illustrated a parable in which a servant was admonished for not putting his master's money to good use – *Thou oughtest therefore to have put my money to the exchangers, and then at my coming I should have received mine own with usury."* Banking in its widest sense is a multi-faceted discipline. A history of such a system therefore needs a specific approach if justice is to be done to any particular area.

The Evolution of Banking in The USA.

The evolution of banking in the United States is punctuated by various colorful incidents on the one hand, and intermittent periods of depression on the other. This lends to an interesting study and interpretation of the events which led to the present form of the banking system in the United States.

This is an attempt to trace banking in the USA from the earliest records. Such a task should yield tangible information which allows us to understand the progressive attraction of ***greed*** through the years. This approach will be confined to a study of banking as an institution, and to the rules that affected its formation over time. Such information will be crucial at a later time as we discuss the Bible's warning about the Antichrist.

The Ancients.

An understanding of the situation which led to the early practice of banking in the United States is incomplete without some insight of banking prior to its recognition in the colonies.

The Assyrians, Babylonians, and Athenians, all transacted business in a fashion that could be considered as banking in its simplest form. John Knox noted in his History of Banking in the United States that, *"Where ever a people were sufficiently advanced to loan money for hire there would naturally spring up many of the practices and methods of modern banking."*[5] It should be noted however, that these ancient businessmen did not have faith in the credit system. It is this factor which mainly differentiates their system from that of modern banking.

The First Real Bank.

The first real banking institution (according to contemporary systems) was founded in Venice during 1171. A *forced* loan was levied on the rich citizens of that Republic. The amount of specie (actual coins) loaned was entered in a book since there was to be an annual return of 4% interest, and records needed to be maintained to allow accurate and timely repayments on the investments. The Republic paid the interest, but never repaid the principal. The citizens therefore made private arrangements to transfer the value, and therefore ensure that they did not lose. They immediately recognized the ease with which this was accomplished in the absence of handling actual specie. The bank was therefore flooded with deposits of specie as people continued to take advantage of private transactions based on the value of their deposits with the bank.

Personal Notes

Other Early Banks.

The experience in Venice caused many other countries to follow that pattern: there was the Bank of Genoa in 1320 where paper notes were issued during the latter part of its existence. The Bank of Amsterdam followed in 1609. These banks failed in 1798 and 1790 respectively.[6]

An English Perspective.

Banking in the United States was not patterned after the system in England during the early years. The Jews were the first bankers in England, having arrived from France in 1066 with William the Conqueror. They used bills of exchange, and accumulated stocks of coins. These they loaned to the nobility and others at a high rate of interest. The loans were secured by lands and estates owned by the borrowers. King Edward I banished the Jews after taking away their wealth. The Lombards of Italy took over the business, and combined their goldsmith and pawn broking activities with banking. [7]

During 1566 a Goldsmith's company was formed in England, and began to perform as bankers in 1645. As bankers they collected rent for their customers, and also received money from them on which interest was paid. When they acted as pawnbrokers, they issued notes which were actually receipts payable on demand (Demand Notes). The use of checks soon followed – customers gave orders on their bank through the checks they wrote.

The Bank of England was formed with the aid of a loan of £1,200.000 to the government on July 27, 1694. This royally chartered bank had to repay the loan at an interest rate of 8%. They obtained periodic renewals of the charter until 1844 when the present law was introduced. [8]

The American Pattern.

It is with the background mentioned above that businessmen in the American colonies sought to perpetuate and solidify monetary transactions. They strove from the inception to create an atmosphere of trust and confidence – they realized that without such faith in the enterprise, any monetary transaction based on credit was doomed to failure. The precepts adopted over the years were

Personal Notes

definitely based on the fact that, *"the business of banking, in its widest sense, is to collect in banks or masses, the capital of a community, that which either is money or can readily be turned into money, and upon the capital so collected, to build up by proper management and machinery, a credit which will extend and enlarge the usefulness to the community of its actual moneyed capital."* [9]

Personal Notes

Early Banking In The American Colonies.

During the 17th century, there were no banks in the American colonies for the purpose of clearing business transactions. This, along with the underdeveloped state of short term credit arrangements, hampered commerce. Coins of a small denomination were in short supply because much of the specie gained from trade with the Spanish and Portuguese was used to pay for imports from England. At that time beaver skins and tobacco were used widely for monetary purposes.

Bills of credit were first used in Massachusetts in 1690 to finance a military expedition against the French in Canada. The issue of paper money was such an attractive prospect that the rest of New England succumbed to this venture by 1712, and also impacted New York, New Jersey, and South Carolina. By 1760 the remaining colonies, with the exception of North Carolina, had also issued paper money. Public Land banks sponsored by each colonial government, except Virginia, were also sources of paper money. [10] It should be noted that the issues of paper money during this time were initially for the benefit of the colonial treasuries – Americans saw banks at that time as being stacks of paper money.

The First Commercial Bank.

The first known commercial bank in the United States was chartered on December 31, 1781. The Bank of North America which commenced operations in Philadelphia on January 7, 1782, was the first permanently organized bank to which the Continental Congress of the thirteen original States had issued a charter on a perpetual basis. The bank claims that the charter is still in effect today. A look at its origin and developments which led to its formation is pertinent to our interest in this study.

Personal Notes

Prior to December 1781, there were other efforts to commence the establishment of an organized banking institution. The revolutionary war effort was a strain on the soldiers because of financial hardship. Thomas Paine, Clerk of the Pennsylvania Assembly, suggested a contribution to ease the plight of the soldiers. Paine enclosed his personal subscription of $500 when he made the suggestion to Mr. Blair McClenachan, a United States Representative, and ardent entrepreneur. This led to a meeting of patriotic citizens on June 7, 1780 at the Coffee House. Messrs. Robert Morris and McClenachan were among those present. It was resolved that a subscription drive should be started, *"To be given in bounties to promote the recruiting service of the United States."* [11]

The first meeting yielded 400 pounds in hard money, and 103,360 in Continental money in nine days. However, these funds were insufficient to meet the needs of the soldiers. Another meeting of the subscribers was summoned for June 17. At this session the original plan was discarded. Instead, it was resolved to open a security *"Subscription to the amount of 300,000 pounds of Pennsylvania currency, in real money."* Bonds were to be executed to the subscribers to the amount of their subscriptions to form the capital of the so called bank.[12] This latter proposal necessitated the introduction of the principles which governed the system of commercial banking.

Amounts ranging from one to ten thousand pounds were subscribed. The quota was attained after ninety two persons gave their subscriptions. The bank was to be known as the Pennsylvania Bank with the following resolutions to guide its operations:

1. 10% of the subscriptions were to be paid at once, and the remainder from time to time as required.
2. Interest bearing Notes were to be issued at 6%.
3. The credit of the bank or association of subscribers was to be used to borrow money.
4. All sums borrowed or received from Congress were to be applied to meeting notes and expenses of the bank, and

Personal Notes

> purchasing and transporting supplies of provisions and rum for the use of the Continental army.[13]

After congress was informed of the above, a committee of three was selected to examine and report on the proposals. Resolutions by this committee were unanimously adopted, *"Accepting the offerings of the associations as a distinguished proof of their patriotism, and pledging the faith of the Government for the effectual reimbursement of the amount advanced."*[14]

Operations of the Pennsylvania Bank commenced on July 17, and lasted for 1 ½ years, eventually winding up affairs toward the end of 1784. Those who had subscribed received bank notes baring interest. This bank had evolved based on the war effort, but it was not given a true charter although its functions were acknowledged by the Government.

The Bank of North America.

During 1781, American trade was in need of organized financial management. Robert Morris, Superintendent of Finances, saw this need, and together with a few influential merchants of Philadelphia, entertained the thought of a commercial bank. On April 30, 1781, Alexander Hamilton wrote to Morris urging the creation of a National Bank. This gave Morris the opportunity to crystallize his original plans. Accordingly, he drew up a plan for the formation of the Bank of North America, and submitted it to Congress on May 26, 1781. Morris' presentation to Congress involved the following particulars:

1. Opening subscriptions should be $400,000 in shares of $400 each, payable in gold and silver (make special note of this factor for future reference).
2. Subscribers of five shares were to pay one half at once, and the remainder in three months.
3. After the capital was paid in, the organization was to be completed.

Personal Notes

4. There were to be twelve directors chosen annually who were to elect one of their number as president, and two others as inspectors to control the affairs of the bank.

5. It was to be a National Bank, and its notes were to be receivable for duties and taxes in each state, and in settlement of accounts between the states and Congress, accepted instead of specie. 15

This system bears a close resemblance to the principles on which present banks operate. Perhaps it was because of this show of thorough planning, and the interest displayed by Hamilton, that several businessmen were prompted to transfer their capital from the Pennsylvania bank to the new enterprise. The main opposition to the plan came from Madison, even though it had favorable appraisal from the committee which examined it. The plan was adopted by Congress after a short deliberation.

On December 31, 1781, a perpetual charter, the first of its kind, was given to the new institution which commenced operations on January 7, 1782. The Bank of North America was then recognized by Connecticut, Rhode Island, New York, and Massachusetts.

Early Operation of The New Bank.

The early operations of the Bank of North America can be considered one of the catalysts which resulted in the formation of other banks during that era. It is therefore meet to trace the early transactions of the bank in order to gain a clearer understanding of the events that followed.

The main reason for the formation of the Bank of North America was based on the need to support the revolutionary war effort. This is despite Morris' original ambitions surrounding trade which governed his previous actions. France, in an effort at retaliation to their defeat by the British in Canada, was assisting the revolutionary efforts of the Americans. Morris received specie to the value of $470,000 from the French. He retained $254,000 which was used to subscribe to 633 shares of the bank's stock. However, by July the exigencies of the Government made him borrow $400,000 from the bank. At this point in its operations, specie in the bank was precariously low. The faith of the Government, and the backing of the business community precluded the bank from failure, and so three years later the situation was completely reversed.

After such a turbulent beginning it was remarkable that within three years the bank was so strong that its notes were current throughout the country at par (stated or face value). This was even more remarkable because the Government was refusing Continental money. This show of strength caused the directors of the bank to increase the stock from $400,000 to $2,000,000. However, this increase was distributed between projectors of a new banking enterprise, mainly to persuade them to desist from such ambitious ventures, the idea of course being to maintain a monopoly in the banking endeavor. This type of maneuver continues to this day – notice the various mergers and sometimes aggressive manipulations within the banking community.

Some Legal Moves

The financial operations of this bank were invariably influenced by various fears. The directors were not satisfied with the perpetual charter obtained from the Congress of the Confederation – they felt that it may not be recognized nationally. This in itself portrays the ultimate ambition of those who were in control of the system at that time. Pay attention to this gradual incursion into every facet of the American society – it is this pervasive power, fueled by the subtle undercurrent of greed that has resulted in our current economic dilemma. But more than that, from a spiritual perspective it ushered in, and set the stage for various misconceptions and fallacies concerning the true purpose and use of money. Ultimately, the devil rides on the back of such folly which only serves to augment his own plans in his attempt to derail God's act of redemption and reconciliation through Jesus' sacrifice on the Cross.

In an effort to quell their fears, the directors sought a similar charter from the Assembly at Pennsylvania. The perpetual aspect seemed repugnant to the Assembly. Nevertheless, the charter was granted on March 26, 1782. This charter was repealed by the State of Pennsylvania in 1785 – mainly through the influence

Personal Notes

Personal Notes

of those who wished to issue more paper money, and saw the bank as a hindrance to their ambitions. Think of it – what happens when there is more paper money than its backing by gold, silver or specie – it's actually worthless. Can you see the invitation to failure? Can you relate this to our current economic situation? Of course you can – the evidence of greed and its painful effects are so poignant, how could you miss it. So many lives around the world have been affected by what initially appeared as a 'good thing,' helping to microwave the American Dream. But be vigilant, if it appears too good to be true, it usually is!

During the period that the Bank of North America had the Charter of Pennsylvania, it was able to operate under two umbrellas, National and State. After the charter was repealed, the bank existed under the National charter only. This prompted the directors to seek another State charter. An application was made to Delaware on February 2, 1786. The overwhelming approval of Delaware caused the Assembly of the Commonwealth to issue a corporate franchise to the bank – note the progression. Meanwhile, there was a change of influence in Pennsylvania. Consequently, in 1787 that State revived the charter to the bank for a period of fourteen years with a capital of $2,000,000.

The tremendous influence of the bank at this time is seen in Hamilton's letter to the Collector of Customs on September 22, 1789. The letter to Otho H. Williams of Baltimore directed him to, *"Receive the notes of the Bank of North America and the Bank of New York, payable either on demand or at no longer period than 30 days after their respective dates, in payment of duties, as equivalent to gold and silver."* [16]

Now the fun begins as the personal interests of influential individuals direct the course of events affecting the banking system. The first session of Congress under the Constitution began on March 4, 1789. The salaries of President Washington, the Senators and Representatives were initially paid by the banks mentioned in Hamilton's letter. But a quest for power soon hampered the smooth operation of the system.

Personal Notes

It should be recalled that the original intent which fostered the formation of the Bank of North America, was National in scope. But the operations of the bank had grown to the extent that there was need to assess its legal position. The acceptance of its last State charter, according to Hamilton, precluded it from being legally recognized as the Bank of the United States. So, even though the Bank of North America was the first bank to deal extensively with Government finances, yet it was not given the signal honor of being the First Bank of the United States.

Toward A National Bank.

The State Charter of the Bank of North America was renewed periodically until 1864. At that time, several State institutions were becoming National banks and were required to change their names at least to the extent of inserting the word 'National.' The exception was the Bank of North America which became a National bank on December 3, 1864. This bank was allowed to retain its original name because of is "Sterling patriotic contribution," to use the words of the Comptroller of Currency, the Hon. Hugh McCulloch. *17*

Commercial Banks – A General View.

The success of the Bank of North America prompted other States to attempt similar exploits. The Bank at Baltimore was among the first to start operations in 1784. The merchants from Boston petitioned on behalf of the Massachusetts Bank and succeeded in 1784 as well. A charter was granted in 1790. In other instances such as in New York, political opposition prevented the bank from receiving a charter before 1791. Nevertheless, it operated in an unincorporated form from as early as 1784.

There were therefore three commercial banks in operation when the Constitutional Convention assembled in 1787. From that period onwards, the formation of commercial banks had a fluctuating pattern which is interesting to follow. Note in particular the Government's influence in banking at that time, and compare it with its recent intervention to save the economy through a 'bail out' for several banks.

The Early Evolution.

The United States had a total of eighteen banks by 1794, and twenty nine by 1800. This included the federally chartered First Bank of the United States with five branches. Five of the first eight banks to be chartered by the various States are still in operation. Twelve of the twenty nine banks listed in 1800 have been in continuous operation for over 185 years.

Between 1834 and 1837, 194 new banks were formed; 62 in New England, 42 in five Middle States, 72 in nine Southern States, and 18 in four Western States. During this time, there was an increase in the issuing of notes; $6,000,000 by the banks of New England States, $14,000,000 by banks of the Middle States, $34,000,000 by those of the South, and $6,800,000 by the banks of the West. These figures do not include amounts from 'Wild Cat' banks, since they did not report to the Secretary to the Treasury.

All such issues were to be backed by adequate specie, gold, or silver. In an effort to ensure the validity of transactions involving the release of notes, President Jackson issued the specie circular through the Secretary of the Treasury on July 11, 1836. This forbade the receipt of anything but specie in payment of the public lands. It's a wonder that some of the banks lasted so long after this effective circular.

Population As A Criterion

Banks began to come out of the wood work. It was obvious that businessmen saw the lucrative potential of this financial institution. However, although the main factor seemed to be the profit motive, yet it will be determined from future events that greed fueled many of the operations. In these early years politics played an essential role in the success or failure of many of these organizations.

It seems that, by and large, the size of a community decided the number of banks it would have. In some instances, however, small communities experienced heavy commercial activity. It appears that this was based on the financial mobility in the area.

Personal notes

Personal Notes

In 1800 there was a bank in every town of New England that had a population of at least 5,000. The exceptions were; Marblehead and Bridgewater in Massachusetts and Norwalk Connecticut. Six communities with less than 5,000 boasted a bank – there were sixteen such banks. The rest of the nation together had thirteen banks – two in areas with populations less than 5,000. Surprisingly, four locations outside of New England with populations in excess of 5,000 did not have a bank – this included Schenectady in New York, the Virginia ports of Norfolk (which did have a branch of the Bank of the United States), Richmond, and Savannah, Georgia. Within the next ten years, the four States without banks in 1800 had each acquired at least one bank; North Carolina and New Jersey in 1804, Vermont in 1806, and Georgia in 1810. *18*

The Battle Begins – Deceptions & Schemes

Particular pains are being taken to highlight the emergence of the banking and other financial institutions in order to establish the effects on society and the economy as a whole. The parallel with our contemporary experiences should make it easier to understand the current state of our financial affairs.

Most banks in the early years attempted to control particular areas. But in the 19th century, progress was so rapid that the need for additional facilities propelled customers to seek new institutions - especially since they were dissatisfied with the operations of the prevailing banks.

Between the years 1791 and 1816 the total number of banks grew from a mere six to two hundred and forty six. In commercial centers, banks backed their operations with a specie capital base as they made short term loans to merchants. These were the wild years – various excuses were made to go into the banking business. An interesting observation is that while specie, gold or silver was used as a capital base in most viable operations, the main or sole capital base in agricultural areas hinged on the State's credit. Now that should strike a note.

During this period, businessmen concealed their true intentions so as to avoid politically motivated opposition to their schemes. For example, such deception was clearly evident in the operations of the Miami Exporting Company

Personal Notes

of Cincinnati, chartered in 1803 to ship farm produce to New Orleans, it immediately went into banking on receipt of the charter. Another example is the Manhattan Company which was chartered in 1799 to provide wholesome water to New York City – they became the Aaron Burr's Bank. [19]

The Free Banking Laws

It was evident that the surge of the banking business was drawing more and more Americans into a greater awareness of the money economy. Consequently, politics played a major role in the success or failure of many ventures. Over the years, commercial banking was plagued with many instances of discriminatory actions and political opposition. The Declaration of Independence, no doubt, prompted forward looking persons to draft similar measures to fit the American banking system, and to eliminate the monopolistic situation which prevailed.

The Free banking Act was introduced in New York in April 1838, and among other things stipulated, *"Any who wished could associate themselves for banking purposes by meeting the specifications of a general law.'* [20] This law was seen as a milestone in American banking history, and established a pattern which was distinctly American. The stipulation was that bank notes were to be secured by bonds of New York and the United States, or by mortgages on New York real estate.

New York was not the first to introduce such a law, but was the first to experience a stable and successful banking environment under these restrictions. Prior to New York's Act, Michigan tried a similar Free Banking law in March of 1837. But the forty banks formed as a result, soon went into receivership – perhaps because the Act was not founded on firm principles which were seen in the New York Act when that came into being. However, as a result of the success in New York, several other States adopted similar measures. Free banking was made a part of the National Banking Act of 1863.

Free Banking, Greed & Deception

Personal Notes

The Free Banking laws of the various States enabled many businessmen to create banking institutions. In some States, the prudential provisions of the New York Act were omitted. This allowed non-residents to open banks in areas where they had no tangible assets. Many bankers disappeared shortly after opening for business – sounds familiar? This state of affairs tarnished the credibility of the banking profession, and prompted the creation of rules by State officials to safeguard individual assets.

In several instances individual businessmen, in an effort to maximize profits, ignored sound banking practices – they extended credit beyond their ability to back and safeguard individual investments. Banks once formed, were able to issue bank notes. The untenable situation which prevailed caused several States to require that banks maintain a legal reserve in order to prevent an over issue of such currency. As early as 1861, the early charters limited the banks to a liability which was some multiple of its (supposedly specie) capital – in effect signifying a legal reserve. The Federal Law of 1863 followed the 1842 statute which specified for the first time a specie reserve of one third for both deposits and bank notes.

Government, Banks, And The Economy

The foregoing clearly identified the need for continued vigilance and regulations by the various State Governments. However, the growth of the Nation and its effect on the general economy also established the need for 'central' control of the movement of money. This latter view was evident even before the firm establishment of the banking industry in the 19th century.

The scarcity of money during the revolutionary days, and the debt created as a result, necessitated swift intelligent remedies by the administration. As early as 1779, Alexander Hamilton saw the need for the establishment of a banking institution to benefit the financial situation of the country. He proposed the formation of "The Company of the Bank of the United States," with a capital of $200,000,000 to be incorporated by Congress for ten years. *21*

Personal Notes

Prior to this move in 1779, there were other circumstances that mitigated in favor of the eventual birth of centralized banking through Banks of the United States. Since the advent of the first Congress in 1774, Continental money was issued in anticipation of taxes to be received through the acts of Congress – note that the money was circulated *before* there was any tangible backing in reserve. This in essence is really how our credit system operates – there is anticipation that loans will be made good. Further, the more persons involved, the greater the potential to give credit. This is based on the assumption that there will never come a time when everyone would make a simultaneous demand on the bank for their money. Well, it may be a reasonable assumption, but our recent experiences demonstrate that the improbable is possible, and financial disaster is the result.

Thomas Jefferson's comments on this precarious situation are worth noting – they give a very clear picture of the dangers, and the quandary the administration experienced – a good lesson for contemporary evaluation. He said, *"At the commencement of the late Revolution, Congress had no money. The external commerce of the States being suppressed, the farmer could not sell his produce, and, of course, could not pay a tax. Congress had no resource then but in paper money. Not being able to pay a tax for its redemption, they could not promise that taxes should be laid for that purpose, so as to redeem the bills by a certain day. They did not foresee the long continuance of the war, the almost total suppression of their exports, and other events which rendered the performance of their engagements impossible. The paper money continued for a twelve month equal to gold and silver; but the quantities which they were obliged to limit for the purpose of war exceeded what had been the usual quantity of the circulating medium. It began therefore, to become cheaper or, as we expressed it, it depreciated, as gold and silver would have done had they been thrown into circulation in equal quantities. But not having, like them, an intrinsic value, its depreciation was more rapid and greater than could ever have happened with them. In two years it had fallen to two dollars of paper money to one of silver; in three years to four for one; in nine months more it fell to ten for one, and, in the six months following, that is to say, by September 1779 it had fallen to twenty for one."*[22]

This is the profound and alarming situation which prevailed and propelled Congress toward a search for means to fund the revolutionary debt. The ingenious scheme of a Bank of the United States was bred out of this chaotic economic atmosphere.

The formation of the Banks of the United States followed the observation above. The first Bank of the United States received a charter from Congress, and commenced business in January 1791. The constitution granted the Federal Government the exclusive right to coin money, and deprived the individual States of a similar function. It also forbade the States from issuing bills of credit. This charter to the First Bank came to an end in 1811 after its legal duration of twenty years expired – it was never renewed.

During 1816, a second Bank of the United States received a similar twenty years charter. This too, was not renewed at the expiration of the period. Nevertheless, the need for some form of centralized control still existed. The stock holders and directors of this second Bank therefore redirected their efforts by accepting a charter from the State of Pennsylvania. This bank also failed in 1841. Thereafter, until February 25, 1863, there was no bank in the United States doing business under Federal law – that is, save and except one or two small institutions doing business in Columbia.

These banks failed because people lacked confidence in them. The Government preferred to do business with the well established State banks during these turbulent years because of their proven patriotism. However, these State banks in which custom duties and other revenues were deposited, proved inadequate for the purpose of the Government's financial transactions – control was limited. In the words of President Van Buren at the opening session in 1837, *Both National and State banks were tried and found wanting as custodians of the Public money."*[23] He recommended legislation by which the Government would take charge of its own funds. This statement was followed by the introduction of a

Personal Notes

bill by Silas Wright of New York proposing an Independent Treasury system. Under this proposal the Treasury would be operated through the oversight of a Treasurer. After some difficulty because of the state of the financial affairs in the economy, the bill finally became law on July 4, 1840. It is worth noting that this system required that after June 30, 1843 all payments to or by the United States should be in gold or silver exclusively. Not surprisingly, the banks attacked this rule vigorously, and it was repealed on August 13, 1841. Subsequently, five months after the inauguration of President Harrison, the Independent Treasury Act was also repealed. But through it all there remained one consensus – the need for some form of central control to safeguard both public and private funds.

The Federal Reserve System – A Synopsis.

Banking in the United States became more and more complex as the years went by. Experiences gained in one period provided the framework for the guidelines of future operations. Many banks were founded without a proper base, and as a result, were doomed to failure from the inception. Depositors had to be careful when investing their funds, since there was no concrete guarantee of safety. The panics which followed various failures were of nationwide consequences. This dictated that the Federal Government should take measures to ensure a perpetually healthy banking environment. It is under these circumstances that the Federal Reserve System came into being.

The Panics.

An overview of the failures of the banking system and the panics which ensued should give a clearer perspective of the reasons for the establishment of the Federal Reserve System.

The first major panic of note occurred in 1837, followed by another twenty years later in 1857. Each President of the respective era, Van Buren and Buchanan, blamed the operations of banks for the financial crises. The extravagant and vicious system of paper currency and bank credits was seen as the major cause of the economic down turn. The problem seemed to stem from the fact that banks were allowed to manufacture the circulating medium of

Personal Notes

exchange, and did not always have the necessary collateral to back their issues. According to Henry Vethake, a University of Pennsylvania economist, the American banking system had not a single redeeming quality about it. He viewed it from the beginning to end as a compound of quackery and imposture.[24] Does this echo your sentiments concerning the current state of our banking system?

The other panic of consequence took place during 1907 despite the relative security which prevailed after the passing of the National Banking Act in 1863. The world wide depression which ensued during 1907, had a profound effect on the American banking system which still retained a few loopholes. Farmers, unable to obtain their money when required, orchestrated the situation which eventually culminated in the Federal Reserve Act of 1913.

The Evolution of the Federal Reserve System.

The National Monetary Commission, established in 1908, had examined and analyzed the various crises. A National Reserve Association was advocated in 1912 – a voluntary, banker dominated organization. However, there was a change in Government before this could be ratified. Nevertheless, the new administration did not discard the plan in its entirety, but modified it. The new plan called for a decentralized Central Bank with shared private and public control. This system, established by legislation in 1913, consisted of member banks, the Federal Reserve Banks, and the Federal Reserve Board.

It was stipulated that all national banks must become members of the Federal Reserve System. They became the operating nucleus of the Federal Reserve Banks. Commercial State chartered banks had the option of remaining aloof or participating. They were usually granted membership once they had adequate capital. During 1979, all banks became members since all banks were directed to maintain a required reserve. There was therefore no distinction between National and State chartered banks, all were now members of the Federal Reserve System. The formation of this Federal Reserve System was engaged to monitor the activities of American banks, and to take measures to avoid another depression. Toward that end, the 'System' comprised of various sections, each

Personal Notes

with particular responsibilities to maintain stability within the banking environment, and hence within the economy as a whole.

Composition of the Federal Reserve System

The Federal Reserve System is managed by a Board of Governors comprised of seven members appointed by the President with the consent of the Senate. Each member serves a tour of fourteen years, but particular circumstances may cause this period to be extended. The exceptions are the Chairman and Deputy Chairman who are each initially appointed for four year terms which can be extended up to the maximum of fourteen years. Individual tours terminate in January of each even numbered year.

The seven members of this Board join with the President of the New York Federal Reserve Bank, and four other Presidents of Reserve Banks who are allowed to serve on a rotating basis for one year terms. Together, they comprise the Federal Open Market Committee. The purpose of this committee is to discuss monetary matters affecting the economy. It is chaired by the Chairman of the Board of Governors for the Federal Reserve System, while the President of the New York Federal Reserve Bank serves as his Deputy.

There is also the Federal Advisory Council which meets four times in each year to discuss economic issues and to offer advice to the Chairman of the Board of Governors. In order to examine the complexities of the American economy and the banking system from various perspectives, this Advisory Committee is made up of twelve commercial bankers, chosen by the Board of Directors of each Federal Reserve Banking district. They are allowed to serve for terms of three years each. This Council was founded under the 1913 Act, while the Federal Reserve Open Market Committee was established through the 1935 Act. It is relevant to note that as a means of uniformity in the Federal Reserve System, the Federal Reserve Banks also have Directors of their own. There are definitive directions as to their composition. According to stipulations of the Federal Reserve Act, each must have a Board comprising nine persons, with diverse

Personal Notes

interests and expertise – representing member banks, borrowing groups, and the Public interest.

Personal Notes

The Federal Reserve System – What It Does

The Federal Reserve System was created to 'keep an eye on things' - to monitor the activities within our American banking system, and so avoid the financial pitfalls and disasters that prevailed in the early years. So, apart from the unique and varied composition of the System, what tangible checks and balances exist from day to day to sound the alarm when necessary? The answer to this question lies perhaps in the seven major services offered by the Federal Reserve System. The system is responsible for:

1. The supplying and reception of currency and coins. This obviously helps, as a monitoring function, to keep a watch on the level of spending in the economy.
2. The clearing of checks. Serves the same purpose as the first.
3. The wire transfer of funds and securities. In addition to the functions mentioned previously, also serves to keep a hand on the pulse of the international market.
4. Giving loans to depository institutions. This serves to retain the balance necessary for a stable economy. We saw this in operation during 2009.
5. Maintaining banks' reserves. This is one of the main trumpets which would sound when financial trouble approaches the horizon.
6. Auditing banks once per year. Again, 2009 demonstrated just how crucial this function can be – various malpractices and dangerous schemes were discovered.
7. Periodically publishing economic bulletins. This serves to keep the various agencies of the economy aware of its state – it's not only for financial institutions, but for the benefit of the general public as well.

MANAGING GOD'S FINANCES

Personal Notes

The Federal Reserve System introduces new rules and regulations from time to time in order to keep abreast of changes in the financial environment. Such actions have served to retain a stabilizing effect on American banking, and consequently on the economy as a whole. Had it not been for these checks and balances, this nation would not now be on the road to economic recovery after the various failures within financial institutions experienced over the last few years.

Conclusion

Banking in the United States has traveled a long economic road, interspersed with both successes and failures. From the time of the simple maneuvers of the goldsmiths and merchants to the present complexities of the modern enterprise, various measures had to be adopted to save the economy from total bankruptcy.

Over the years the role of Government in banking took tremendous leaps, until finally, depositors are assured of the lasting and trustworthy nature of the banking institution, or so it seems. Is this environment truly what it appears to be, relatively safe, or is this a false sense of security which is intended to lull us unsuspectingly into the next and final phase of chaos, both natural and spiritual?

The two chapters that follow should serve to pinpoint the economic danger zones within the banking system, but from a Biblical and prophetic platform. Let's see how all this "secular stuff" is relative to Satan's continued ploy to derail us from observing sound Christian financial management of God's funds, and hence the financial support of His plan for the redemption of humankind.

MANAGING GOD'S FINANCES

Chapter 9

MOVING TOWARD A CASHLESS SOCIETY – THE DANGERS

Personal Notes

Towards a cashless society? How ludicrous, we will always need cash, or would we? For a moment, we were astonished until we had an opportunity to reflect on the words of Rev. 13:16-18. We are advised through John that a time will come when we can neither buy nor sell unless we carry a particular mark. Are we approaching such a time? If so, are we doing what is essential and necessary to ensure that our relatives and others have an opportunity to join in the *'Rapture of the Saints,'* and so avoid the catastrophe of the *'Mark of the Beast?'* Saints, the writing is on the wall!

From Stash To Cash.

In the 'Good Old Days,' people stored their wealth at home in the form of silver and gold. They did not trust institutions to keep their treasures. Do you recall the term 'specie' used in the previous chapter? It is representative of coins in hard silver or gold. Very much like the population at large, banks wanted tangible assets to back their investments. Wherever this was lacking, the banks eventually failed.

Today, there are Federal Reserve Laws which govern the situation. But even these laws seem to lack the power against greed – an issue which is really behind many of the economic difficulties experienced by this nation and other so-called developed countries. According to Federal Reserve law, banks must keep in reserve the equivalent of the deposits they lodged with the Federal Reserve System. But it is instructive to know that even the Federal Reserve is no longer what it is supposed to be – our gold reserve is not a true reflection of the value of our dollar in present circulation. In other words, the amount of gold in the Federal Reserve is not enough to back the U.S. currency in the market, thus weakening the American dollar. We all know that the Government has been battling for some time to correct this untenable situation. But the difficulty of this state of affairs was brought home forcefully when we recently experienced the collapse, or near collapse of many banks, and automobile merchants. From what was said before, you can envisage that the Government's bailout is only a temporary 'fix.' Unless some concrete effort is made to revive the value of the dollar by ensuring a tangible and equivalent reserve, all efforts will be futile. In our current process, we are gradually, but systematically being pushed toward a state of less reliance on actual physical cash.

The Technique.

The various corrective measures introduced to the nation, in themselves appear to be for the benefit of the people, and toward greater efficiency. However, since the issue surrounds money and the quality of life, one must be assured that there is no sinister agenda behind the introduction of these innovative devices.

Today we are aware of the following items which have greatly reduced the use of actual cash:

1. The ATM/Debit card. We frequently use this card to transact financial matters without the physical use of cash. I call this the 'Cross-over' card since we can also use it to obtain cash even when the banks are closed for official business.
2. On-line Banking. We are able to gain access to our bank records from our personal computers at home. Creditors can be paid electronically through this system, and the physical movement of cash is curtailed.
3. Credit cards. These allow us to purchase goods and services without the use of cash. The debit card is also used for this purpose when we desire that payment should be made directly from our checking account, instead of incurring further debt through a credit card.

Special Cases.

We are walking around today with less money than in years gone by. In this position we can examine some more startling devices which need specific attention. For example, I am paid accurately each fortnight without having to go

Personal Notes

through the usual cumbersome payroll procedures. Each day, staff enter the last six digits of their Social Security number into a computerized Digital Hand Reader, and their palms on the flat surface of the device. This works in a similar fashion as fingerprinting machines, and records the individual's time of arrival and departure (the same process is engaged at the end of the work day). This computer linked process serves to calculate wages, and to make related electronic deposits into bank accounts where required. Talk about sophistication, well here it is. But do you see the dangers in this? Staff had no say in the introduction of this system – the Administration was the sole controlling factor. Should I disagree? There is no problem with the system – yet. But even if I disagreed, I would certainly have to seek another job. Now here is the observation. What if it was the 'Mark' that was being introduced instead? The point is that this could very well represent the subtle manner by which the real atrocity may be introduced.

Then there is the Government's proposed consolidation of the information contained in various crucial cards such as our Social Security, Immigration, Health Care, and Driver's license to name a few. The explanation is that this would serve to enhance the benefits attributable to these cards. But it seems to me that this would give the Government the ability to tabulate and synchronize information about every American individual. The long term effects of such a system can be the loss of total privacy while fortifying the Government's move toward complete control of our lives. But that would be smoke – the fire is yet to come.

Where Are We Going?

I believe that our current experiences with the various cards are preparing us to accept the ultimate assault of the Devil. It is believed that this Government already has a bio-chip the size of a grain of rice which can easily be inserted under the immediate surface of the skin. All necessary information related to an individual could be contained in this chip. It is easy to speculate that with a "New World Order," individuals could be forced to accept this chip since it would be necessary to enable the purchase of goods and services. We could be fooled into

Personal Notes

believing that the chip is just a progressive development that serves to replace the many cards that we previously used. The convincing observation is that we would no longer have to be concerned with losing cards, or the theft of our information.

By now it should be clear why banks are placing such emphasis on our use of cards and other cashless devices. The average banker may quite innocently be viewing this strategy as a cost efficient way of enhancing his bank's profits, while at the same time providing a safer and convenient atmosphere for his customers. But we shall see later that it is possible that there are some influential people controlling this issue from behind the scenes. It is these hidden commanders who are leading us into a war that will eclipse all other wars.

It is said that he who controls the wealth, controls our lives. More reason for us to ensure that our treasures are laid up in heaven! With God Himself as our Banker, our lives would be under Perfect Control. We would be managing His finances in a manner that pleases Him. However, if our treasures are laid up on earth, it would be easier for us to fall prey to the subtle control of the adversary, and hence ultimate damnation for eternity. Saints, we need to be Awake, and Aware!

Personal Notes

MANAGING GOD'S FINANCES

Chapter 10

CHRISTIANS BEWARE!

Personal Notes

This subject area is so vast, that I will be unable to do more than introduce the main topic – exposing some of the various dangers we face at this time. Although we are confined to a money related discussion, yet the rich scope of this data dictates that the interested reader should seek complementary reading material if greater details are desired. I have chosen to dwell on the influence of some men in Global Financial Affairs, and their impact on the course of Biblical history.

The following is a synopsis of the salient points raised by J.R. Church in his book, "Guardians of the Grail – and the men who plan to rule the world." This book contains a wealth of information which, in my humble opinion, every concerned Christian should know. It sets the stage for a clearer understanding of the present financial climate in which we now exist.

The Lie.

It all started with a myth. Jesus Himself told us that the Devil is the father of lies. There should be no surprise therefore, that the Devil's greatest coup – the tribulation, should evolve through a lie.

According to some sources, Jesus did not die on the Cross. I am sure that many of us have heard this falsehood before. It is said that he feigned death, and was later stolen from the tomb. It was further claimed that He became the husband of Mary Magdalene, and fathered her children. Regardless of your personal views, it is relevant to observe that there are those who actually believe this.

Further to the above, it is believed by some that in 70 A.D, Mary Magdalene fled to France during the Roman destruction of the Temple at Jerusalem. There in France, her offspring married into the royal family, and eventually produced a king of the Merovingian dynasty. **The bottom line here is that if this account is true, then these members of the French Royal family**

Personal Notes

could claim descent from our Lord Jesus. Although false, we will see later that this is the base from which it is believed that the Antichrist will gain power.

Several developments occurred through the ensuing years. The Roman Emperor, Constantine became the first Christian Emperor in 324 A.D, and so caused a division in the Roman Empire. But after his death, one of the French kings – Clovis, was favored and elected by the Pope. This reestablished the control of the mythical dynasty. They became leaders of the Empire. Most of the ruling families of Europe have stemmed from this dynasty.

The Christian Crusades.

The most important development came as a result of the Christian Crusades. These were intended to free Jerusalem from the Muslims. The French played a great role in this activity. The City was taken by 1061, and a French nobleman, Godfroi de Bouillon was chosen as "King of Jerusalem." It is said that he formed a secret organization called 'Ordre de Sion,' today called 'Prieure de Sion.' The Knights Templar was created as a front to legitimize the activities of this clandestine organization. Their main function was supposed to be the protection of visiting pilgrims from marauders who lurked in the way. But it is widely believed that they spent the next nine years digging and plundering the Temple for its wealth. In any case, on their return to France they were all wealthy men. This wealth they began to use to take control of world affairs and to dominate the course of financial history.

Toward World Domination.

The Prieure de Sion under guise of the Knights Templar, introduced an international banking organization that loaned money – gold, to kings and governments around the world. They soon became so powerful that they ignored the authority of the Pope and other leaders. This arrogance signaled their demise, but the Prieure de Sion, the real power, lived on. Many modern organizations can be traced back to the Prieure. It may be surprising to learn that some respected institutions innocently, or knowingly adopted certain titles e.g., The grade of Templar in some Masonic lodges, the De Molay Society – a fraternal organization named after Jacques De Molay who was the 14th century Grand Master of the Knights Templar, Mormonism with a philosophical connection to the ancient Templars, and the Nazi party of 19th century Germany.[25]

Personal Notes

It was mentioned earlier that many of the royal families across Europe are of the Merovingian dynasty which claims ancestry from the line of Jesus. Significantly, many of these families hold influential positions in the banking industry, and control many of the events from behind the scenes. We need to note, for example, that Otto Von Habsburg of Austria held the title of Duke of Lorraine and king of Jerusalem. In January 2007 he made his son Karl, born in 1961, Head of his House. The Luxembourgs have control of the giant computer known as the "Beast," and located in Luxembourg, Belgium. This computer has been built to control the "One World" monetary system. Significantly it is located a mere 100 miles from Brussels, the headquarters of the European Common Market and NATO. [26]

The following is of such importance that it merits quoting from Mr. Church's book – *"Currently, all banking systems throughout Europe and America are connected to the giant computer system. Since its inception, all Social Security records and all military records have been entered into it. Its secret, but likely purpose is to help implement the new one-world monetary system, which will one day soon be a reality by the merging of European and United States currency into a common currency. How simple it would be for the coming world dictator to be able to enslave and control earth's billions through a sophisticated computer fashioned in his likeness. He would have all the facts at his fingertips on every member of the human race and know who receives his orders, obeys his commands and honor his laws."*[27]

Now, how does this all fit into the scheme of things? Well, believe it or not, the Bible spoke of these things in Daniel, chapters 2, 7, and 11, as well as in Revelation 13:7. There is a conspiracy which will lead to a one-world Government. We are presently experiencing the gradual decline of the American dollar, all being engineered from behind the scenes by a few influential men – if we accept Mr. Church's views. Yes, sometimes things are not what they seem to be; despite the financial gurus pronouncement that the American economy is on the rebound, there are factors which can bring it crashing down in an instant.

Most of us wonder how Governments find it difficult to clothe and feed their citizens, yet produce enormous sums of money to fund destructive war efforts. Can it all be a plot to control, and or destroy the masses? From the 1870s unto the panic in 1893, the American economy took a beating. It seems to have been as a result of direct pressure from International Bankers, eager to cripple the economy.

Locally, a combination of J.P. Morgan and Company, with the Rockefeller family business, could control the economic life of this nation, at least to the Federal level. The former Chase Manhattan Bank (now J.P. Morgan Chase Bank) is a merger of the Rockefeller Chase Bank and the Warburg's Manhattan Bank. It was a member of this same Warburg family from Germany, James Warburg, who on February 7, 1950 stood before the American Senate and said, *"We shall have world government whether we like it or not. The only question is, whether the world government will be achieved by conquest or consent."*[28]

The Final Link.

The final connection is established when we trace the subtle incursion of the original International Banker, Mayer Amschel Rotschild, into the economy of the nations. He was born in Germany in 1743 and had five sons. He strategically placed each of them in key European countries to set up Banking Houses. There was one each in Frankfurt, Vienna, London, Paris, and Naples. They loaned European Governments huge sums of money. The scheme was to cause those Governments to repay the national debts by levying taxes against the people. *"By 1850, the House of Rotschild represented more wealth than all the royal families of Europe and Britain combined. The House of Warburg and the House of Rotschild, along with a few other powerful banking houses, became known as International Bankers. They now control the currencies of all the countries of the world."*[29]

Personal Notes

Personal Notes

These are the men who are controlling the banking industry today. Reflect on James Warburg's arrogant statement to the Senate in 1950 concerning world government, and you have a picture of the reason for many of the innovative devices being introduced into the banking system. These are the men who are leading us toward the cashless society mentioned in the previous chapter. Now we see the connection. Those who control the banks, control our lives. It would be a simple thing for them to force people to take that bio-chip implant – potentially, the "Mark of the Beast."

CONCLUSION

The credit cards, Debit cards, ATM cards, Electronic Funds Transfer, and On-line banking, are all convenient and excellent innovations. But we need to remain vigilant and alert to avoid any subtle changes that could lead to bondage. The clandestine rulers of the world are in position. It all started with a lie, but the truth which we know will set us free. I hope that we can understand the need now, more than ever, to alert our relatives and friends to these dangers. Perhaps our sharing will cause them to respond positively to God's call for repentance. We serve a great God who knows how to deliver the godly out of temptation, and to reserve the unjust unto the Day of Judgment to be punished (2 Pet. 2:9). Saints, let us pray. Christians Beware!

MANAGING GOD'S FINANCES

Chapter 11

THE Y2K SCARE AND THE CHURCH

Personal Notes

It is commonly said that hindsight is 20/20. In retrospect, when we recall the issues surrounding the transition from 1999 to 2000, we each probably have a good chuckle. But at the time of the event, no one was laughing – some people were scared out of their wits. The question is, what have we, as Christians learned from the experience?

Today it is recognized that most concerns about Y2K were legitimate. However, there were those who took the opportunity to exploit the masses, and to create a panic in order to foster that exploitation. Every day someone advanced some new theory of gloom and doom – even in the midst of what appeared to be one of America's finest economic moments. Many Christians got caught up in the fear of the 'World' and neglected to strike a balance between what the Bible predicted, and the man made dilemma that threatened our world with potential hazards as the new millennium approached. Remember how we flocked the supermarkets and hardware stores for food and emergency supplies to tide us over? Remember your anxiety when the day approached and you were told that a particular item was sold out? Some people made a lot of money out of that Y2K Scare!

There was enough tangible evidence to support our concern. However, as Christians we needed to be vigilant in order to avoid the snare of fear caused by those who were in the subtle employ of the devil. Remember, 2 Tim. 2:7 – fear does not come from God. Our responsibility at that time, even as it is now in our current economic crisis remains the same. It demanded a careful study of the situation, and applying Biblical truths to evaluate our individual positions, and consequently the actions we should adopt to overcome adverse circumstances.

What Did We Observe?

All of the Y2K problems envisaged centered on our 'advanced' civilization. The computer age has served to lock us into total dependency on the

Personal Notes

relevant technology. Every aspect of our lives is in some way affected by the use of a computer! Thank God that He gave us the ability to create and to be innovative. So in the long run what appeared to be a potential catastrophe was averted by planning, testing, and implementing technological and practical strategies prior to the transition.

At this point, there should be one salient factor tugging at the curious heart of anyone reading this book – how much did this all cost? I will tell you if you promise not to get angry. It was reported that the Federal Government spent $7.2 billion (not the final figure). AT&T spent over $600 million, and Merrill Lynch over $400 million. Britain loaned $500 million to Russia. There were entire nations who could not afford the cost of necessary preparation. But the need for survival caused the economically strong to help the weak – the problem was interrelated – if one arm went down, it had the potential to take the entire body along with it. According to the periodical INFORMATION WEEK dated February 01, 1999, Issue 719, the World Bank loaned Argentina $30 million, Sri Lanka $29 million, and considered giving Malaysia $100 million. Forty five other countries received grants totaling over $7 million with 17 more countries being eligible for a further $3 million.

It's a Money Issue!

The technical problem revolved around the need to change the date on all equipment. But essential to our study is the observation that regardless of the technical problem, money would be required every step of the way. Where did this money come from, especially since in America, the Federal Reserve really could not back the dollar fully? In other words we were using 'Fiat' money as mentioned in chapter 8. The experiences of Y2K demonstrated that in a global crisis money could be found to meet our needs. Are we victims of a skillfully crafted economic lie? Science says nothing is ever destroyed. We know from our study so far that what God created has not diminished. The issue is simply one of inequitable distribution. So the question remains – how can we benefit from the Y2K episode?

A Learning Tree For Christians.

Personal Notes

Many of us no doubt spent money that could have been channeled elsewhere – but for the fear and panic. Was it right to take precautions? Most definitely. But we also needed to be cognizant of the various pitfalls which led to unnecessary expenditure. We needed to follow an old Arabian saying "Trust God, but tie your camel." Although God is the author and finisher of our faith, we should always take sensible precautions in adverse circumstances.

How does this all relate to our current situation you may ask? Well, the same fear that gripped many Christians concerning the advent of Y2K, is gripping them now in our economic down turn. The difference is that whereas money seemed to flow freely then, there is a conservative flow now. Everyone who has a job is walking softly. The banks have tightened up their credit policies, people are losing their homes, and the potential for financial disaster seems to be lurking around the corner.

But the same God that brought us through Y2K, will bring us through now. He did not give us a spirit of fear, but one of power, love, and a sound mind. Let us therefore use those traits to overcome every obstacle we may have to face. These are exciting times to be alive as a Christian – the opportunities to gain legitimate wealth are enormous.

Instead of being mortified by fear, we need to recognize the avenues of increase. Remember, it all begins with a decision to ban fear. Doing so will lead to creative energy. Once the energy is released, we need to be disciplined in order to traverse the bridge of success. Although opportunity will come in overalls looking like work, we should not shun, but grasp it. All will be made possible if we acknowledge the presence of the Holy Spirit, inviting us to let Him help us to manage God's finances.

MANAGING GOD'S FINANCES

Chapter 12

THE ROLE OF THE HOLY SPIRIT *THEN!*

Personal Notes

There is no feasible way to determine conclusively why we need to manage God's finances in the absence of a discussion on the role of the Holy Spirit! Before the managers (humankind) were created, the Holy Spirit was hovering over the deep (Gen. 1:1) – waiting for word from the Word to go into action. He has been here ever since. Throughout history, His wisdom was seen in the successful application of His directions by those who obeyed Him in managing their financial affairs.

God's overall plan is to effect a reconciliation with His creation (2 Cor. 5: 18, 19). Wealth (money) has always been an essential element of that plan. The Holy Spirit who convicts us of sin, and hence toward reconciliation, also functions as our guide and helper toward the successful management of God's material substance entrusted to our care.

Israel was the initial conduit through whom God planned our reconciliation (Rom. 2:10). Beginning with Abraham, Isaac and Jacob, the Holy Spirit guided their economic affairs so that they each obtained and retained material wealth. He instilled in Abraham the wisdom to give tithes to Melchizedek (Gen. 14: 19, 20) and therefore paved the way for the successful management of his financial affairs – tithing is a management tool. He instilled dread into the hearts of both Pharaoh and Abimelech (Gen. 12:14-20; 20:1-16) – they each on separate occasions, were about to interrupt God's divine plan through intimacy with Sarah. But this situation was turned around for Abraham's good as the Holy Spirit intervened, and warned both men of the consequences if they interfered with the future of Israel (paraphrase). Abraham was compensated handsomely on both occasions, and the coffers for reconciliation took another boost.

It was the Holy Spirit who impressed Isaac to resist fear, and unlike his father Abraham, refrain from fleeing to Egypt, but rather plant in the land of famine. His faithfulness enabled him to enjoy a bountiful harvest. It was the Spirit of God who changed Jacob from being a supplanter and deceiver into a man of faith and trust in God. Even his conniving uncle, Laban, unknowingly assisted God's plan with his deception – it took his two daughters, Leah and Rachael to produce the fathers of the tribes of Israel – God's chosen model to lead the way back to Him. In every situation from Abraham to Jacob, the wealth of others was transferred to them in demonstration of God's love (Prov. 13:22) and in particular, His faithful observance of His covenant which would serve to reconcile us to Him (Gen. 12: 1, 2).

Later in this story, when Israel was enslaved by the Egyptians, it was the Holy Spirit that softened the hearts of the Egyptians to release their wealth, while emboldening the children of Israel to demand it. They left Egypt with both severance and back pay for all the years of unpaid slavery (Ex. 12: 35, 36). While in the wilderness, He showed Israel the penalty for misusing His gold – wealth that was intended for a different purpose. The rebels who built a golden calf as a replacement for the true God, were wiped out (Ex. 32:26 – 28). When Balaam covenanted with the kings to curse Israel for money, the Holy Spirit saw to it that only words of blessing proceeded from his mouth (Num. 22:36; 23:5-12). There was a strict policy concerning the use of His wealth. The Holy Spirit would not allow anything to divert funds meant for the work of the ministry. When Ananias and Sapphira kept back part of the price of the land they sold, and lied about it, they were wiped out (Acts 5). During the early stages of the banking industry in the 1800s and early 1900s, banks that lacked integrity of purpose were wiped out. The observation is that those who followed the directions of the Holy Spirit were able to manage their finances successfully – those who didn't were wiped out.

The other side of Israel's financial management was seen in the building of the tabernacle in the wilderness. Here God was demonstrating the true purpose for His wealth. First, He gave Moses elaborate and specific instructions on the construction of this unique vehicle which provided His presence. Then the Holy Spirit worked with the people of Israel who had a willing heart to give into this

Personal Notes

remarkable work. Once more He was creating an environment in which everyone would have fellowship with Him. Back then it was still an indirect relationship, since the masses relied on the priests to initiate contact and fellowship with God on their behalf. But for our purposes, it was their willingness to contribute, and the purpose it served that impacts our view of God's plan of reconciliation in its progression (Ex. 25:8). Under the directions of the Holy Spirit (Ex. 31:1-6) Bezaleel and Aholiab utilized the contributions of gold and other precious items to build the Bridge back to God. In contemporary estimates, Israel contributed what would now be worth millions of dollars. The Holy Spirit uses their history, including the building of the golden calf and this event, to demonstrate the true purpose of God's wealth. Those who follow the directions of the Holy Spirit, will embrace sound financial management. Those who misuse His funds will endure hardships. It is all geared toward reinstating fellowship with the Creator.

The Holy Spirit has been very active through the ages to ensure that we understood the use of wealth in our march back to God. It is no wonder that Jesus, the personification of God Himself, anointed by the Holy Spirit, belabored the relevance of economic issues in God's plan of redemption and reconciliation. The importance of sound financial management cannot be overemphasized. I believe that it was the anointing in Jesus' presence that caused that little boy to give up his lunch, and enabled 5,000 persons to be fed through a miracle. What is interesting, however, is the return on his investment – he got eleven baskets of food for his one. The lesson here as in previous examples, is that there is a benefit for the willing contribution to God's ministry of reconciliation. Zachaeus was so convicted by the Spirit of God, that he restored His ill gotten gain with interest to those he had robbed (Luke 19:1-9). Jesus responded by stating that salvation had arrived at Zachaeus' house. Cornelius, a Roman centurion, got a personal touch from the Holy Spirit because he was in obedience to God's plan – he managed God's wealth by appropriately giving alms when he could. Consequently, he had the honor of being the first recorded gentile to be converted and reconciled (Acts 10). Once more, the proper use of God's wealth brings about a just reward –

Personal Notes

obedience to the guidance of the Holy Spirit serves as the compass that keeps us on course.

What can we conclude about the role of the Holy Spirit back then? It should be evident from our discussion that He had to be strict in enforcing God's progressive plan toward reconciliation. There was a free flow of wealth, and hence the need to ensure that it was maintained in the right hands for the intended purpose. Israel served as God's model of management, and gave the world a perfect view of both the positive and negative implications of handling God's wealth. The Holy Spirit was demonstrating through Israel, and later through the rest of the saved world, ***why*** we need to manage God's finances according to His directions – it is an instrument through which reconciliation will be facilitated. Now we need to observe His directions on ***how*** to manage according to His principles, ensuring that we remain obedient to His plan.

Personal Notes

MANAGING GOD'S FINANCES

PART II

SOME KINGDOM METHODS TO MANAGE GOD'S FINANCES

And the Lord said, "Who then is that faithful and wise steward, whom his lord shall make ruler over his household, to give them their portion of meat in due season? Blessed is that servant whom his lord when he cometh shall find so doing. Of a truth I say unto you, that he will make him ruler over all that he hath." Luke 12:42-44.

MANAGING GOD'S FINANCES

Chapter 13

MONEY AND THE UNFOLDING PROPHESIES
(THIS GENERATION)

In this time of uncertainty, turmoil, and seemingly more questions than answers, Jesus is speaking to us the same words He spoke to His concerned disciples who inquired about the sign of His return, and the end of the world. *"Take heed that no man deceive you. For many shall come in my name, saying, I am Christ; and shall deceive many. And ye shall hear of wars and rumors of wars; see that ye be not troubled; for all these things must come to pass, but the end is not yet. For nation shall rise against nation, and kingdom against kingdom; and there shall be famines, and pestilences, and earthquakes, in divers places. All these things are the beginning of sorrows ……… Now learn a parable of the fig tree; when his branch is yet tender, and putteth forth leaves, ye know the summer is nigh; so likewise ye, when ye shall see all these things, know that it is near, even at the doors. Verily I say unto you, this generation shall not pass, till all these things be fulfilled." (Matt. 24:4-8, 32-34).* Are these prophesies now unfolding before our very eyes – is this the generation Jesus referred to? What has money and its management got to do with this?

Unfolding Prophesies.

One only has to open the newspaper or listen to news over the radio or television, and it seems as though each of them is saturated with evil tidings of various disasters. Day after day the only change is the escalation of these tragedies. Earthquakes taking the lives of thousands, floods in China, wars and famines in Africa, genocide or 'ethnic cleansing' in Europe, to name a few. Many men of God have studied these phenomena in relation to Bible prophesies, and have put together a wealth of information for our instruction. This book draws on a few of these for a clearer understanding of our present position.

Personal Notes

Personal Notes

We have experienced plagues and various deadly infectious diseases killing millions of people all over the world. Today several of these diseases have mutated to the extent that the medical profession is hard pressed to cultivate remedial treatment. Sounds to me like Jesus spoke on these things. The striking importance to this present age are some of the prophecies Jesus referred to, originally voiced by Daniel. These prophesies, in part, speak of a new Roman Empire.

In Daniel 2, we read of the toes of iron and clay. These are representative of the alliance between European nations – fostering the rise of the Antichrist. Where are we now you ask? Well, look at what's happening in Europe. We know that the European Community is stronger now than it has ever been before. They now have a mutual army, and believe it or not, a common currency called the Eurodollar. It was reported as well, that before his passing on November 11, 2004, Yasser Arafat, Chairman of the PLO, met with European leaders in Russia. Combine these events with the prevalence of the natural disasters, and one must wonder how much longer before He comes!

Dr. Jack van Impe in his Sept/Oct 1995 article entitled *"New World Order,"* observed that we could know that we are close to the end by focusing on Israel. Jesus Himself made mention of Israel in the parable of the fig tree (Israel). Based on that prophesy, all significant developments were a spin off from Israel's return to nationhood in 1948.

There were three events of note in 1948 relative to our study: Israel became a nation; there was the inaugural meeting of the European Union – this, it is believed, will lead to the revival of the Roman Empire – the political basis for one-world government. Finally, there was also the formation of the World council of Churches which would help to lay the foundation for a one- world religious system of the Antichrist described in Revelation 13:11 and 17:9.[30]

The Devil made several attempts through various men of power over the years to establish dominion over the world. But their success was in stealing, killing, and destroying. They could not preempt God's plan of salvation – the

Word has to be preached to all nations before that notable day of the Lord comes. Nebuchadnezzar, Cyrus, Alexander The Great, Julius Caesar, Charlemagne, the Muslim Caliphs, Napoleon, Hitler, and Stalin, all failed at their quest for world dominion. But is the time now ripe for such a man to emerge?

Dr. Henry Spaak, former Secretary General of NATO, once said, *"What we want is a man of sufficient stature to hold the allegiances of all people and to lift us out of the economic morass into which we are sinking. Send us such a man, and be he god or devil, we will receive him."(Dan. 11:36; 2 Thess. 2:4).*[31] Walter Cronkite is alleged to have said that we are in a leaderless world. Economist Julian Snyder reportedly said that we have a rendezvous with a world dictator and his appearance may be soon. Now *you* are thinking – are we there?

Are We That Generation?

The Bible tells us that the generation which witnesses the return of Jerusalem into Jewish custody would not pass until the fulfillment of end-time prophecy – Luke 21:24, 31, and 32. Well, Israel was reborn in 1948, and Jerusalem was recaptured in 1967. If we accept what most Biblical scholars believe – that a biblical generation is forty years, then it is reasonable to assume that the time of Jesus' return is near. Although no one knows the actual time or hour, save the Father, yet we can discern the season through the witness of the "Fig Tree."

Dr. Van Impe puts it all together in his November/December 1995 issue of *"Perhaps Today."* He wrote, *"No other period in human history has witnessed so many threats to the survival of the human race. Never before has the stage been so well set for the Second Coming. The geopolitical alliances have been forged. The climatic conditions are in evidence. The spiritual status of the world is just what we would expect. Think about our world today:*

> *Major Christian denominations have been captured by those who reject the essential truth of the Bible and the deity of Jesus Christ. 2 Peter 2:1-3.*
>
> *Bible believing Christians are openly persecuted for their beliefs – by government, by other religious leaders, sometimes even by so-called ministers of the gospel. John 16:2.*

Personal Notes

Personal Notes

There is rampant interest in and acceptance of Eastern religions, extra sensory-perception, astrology, witchcraft, and false prophets. 1 Timothy 4:1, Revelation 9:20.

We see a serious movement toward a one-world religious system, with Pope John Paul II himself fearing the rise of the "anti-Christ" and an anti-Pope in the very near future. Revelation 13:1, 11, and Revelation 17:9.

Israelis talk openly about the imperative to rebuild the Temple in Jerusalem. Ezekiel chapters 40 – 48.

The Middle East remains a constant source of tension and probably flashpoint for a future world war. Ezekiel 38:1,2,15,16.

The U.S. is abdicating its preeminent leadership position in the world in favor of multilateralism, globalization and interdependence. Revelation 13:7.

Europe moves toward unification and the rest of the world is forming regional military and economic alliances that will make eventual global convergence inevitable. Daniel 7:8, 20, 23, 24.

Like never before, people all over the world are looking and yearning for a leader to bring them together. Daniel 11:36.

The worst famines the world has ever known are breaking out. Revelation 6:5, 6.

New epidemics of old plagues are spreading and new diseases are ravaging the planet, even as modern medicine and technology should be overcoming such maladies. Luke 21:11.

Moral chaos in America is tearing apart the fabric of our society. Revelation 9:21.

Drug addiction and abuse are escalating as major problems in America and throughout the Western world. Revelation 18:23.

Crime, riots, unemployment, poverty, illiteracy, mental illness, illegitimacy and other social problems are on the increase. Matthew 24:12."[32]

It seems to me that we are in the generation Jesus spoke about. What do you think?

MANAGING GOD'S FINANCES

Personal Notes

What About Money and Its Management?

You may recall that in the previous chapter, we discussed the clandestine operations of the men with power, and related their activities to the world's banking system. Their potential to dominate this world's economy is directly connected to their wealth. Similarly, every situation mentioned in this chapter has a cost associated with it. The need for financial expenditure is tied in to almost every facet of our existence.

Governments and wealthy organizations are spending millions to find solutions to our various social and political ills. Billions are being spent in cash or kind to avert or to alleviate the wide spread famines or the aftermath caused by natural disasters. The Pentagon unveiled a $10 million reconnaissance plane with uncanny sensitivity – it can detect a basketball on the ground from 45,000 feet (8.5 miles) even in bad weather. There goes our privacy! Revelation 13:16-18. But of greater importance at this time is the global effect of recent monetary decisions by some leading nations.

In another article of *'Perhaps Today,"* October 1998, Dr. Van Impe reported that the European Union continues its growth and influence as the revised Roman Empire predicted in scripture. He wrote that the ECU is preparing to install a unified European currency. Martin Feldstein, Professor of Economics at Harvard University, said in the influential journal *Foreign Affairs*, that a European single currency could cause wars between ECU member states, and lead to disputes between the U.S. and Europe. Another significant report was made by Andrew Craig of *Tech Web News*. He said then that cash will be replaced almost entirely by electronic cards in Europe within the next three years. He went on to say that America would not be far behind – in our case the change will be driven by our widespread use of the internet for making purchases. Time has proven him correct, the current state of affairs indicate that we are moving rapidly in that direction – an indication that he was on the right track. He also said that the Asia-pacific region would follow shortly thereafter as well with the change toward cashless transactions. Revelation 13:16-18.[33]

Personal Notes

An article in the New York Daily News of Thursday May 6, 2010 titled *Huge protests break out as Greece approves drastic budget cuts,* and written by Helen Kennedy, talked about the rampage against the government and banks in Greece. In the words of Kennedy *"Greece's economy is bankrupt and the euro bailout is contingent on austerity measures that require deep cuts in public pensions and tax hikes…… The cuts are vastly unpopular: Ordinary people feel they are being made to pay for the mistakes and corruption of fat-cat financiers and politicians….. Fears that Greek debt problems will be "contagious" – undermining the euro and spreading weakness – were hurting markets globally. The rating agency Moody's warned that Portugal, Italy, Spain and Ireland could be next to face a crisis."*[41] Can you see the strategy of the European Union, and connect that to our discussion?

Joining The Dots.

The crisis just mentioned is a complex manifestation of historical events that occurred several years previously. The gestation period is over, now greed is giving birth to a financial dilemma that cannot be easily reversed. Suffice it to say that the final march to Armageddon has begun.

According to Michael Lewis, writing for the New York Times in September 2011, this debt crisis in Europe is, to some extent, the globalization of finances; the easy way loans were distributed between 2002 – 2008, fueling lending and borrowing with high risk implications; the global recession between 2008-2012; the unhealthy real estate balloon that was pricked by that recession; and the way international governments addressed these issues. [34]

The European Union (EU) via its Central Bank (ECB), continues to make efforts to bail member countries out of the economic chaos. Initially, 750 billion euro dollars were made available on May 9, 2010, and an additional amount of 130 billion in February 2012. Recently, as late as June 6, 2012, a bailout package of 40 to 100 billion euro dollars for Spain was under consideration. So far, recipients of aid from the ECB include Greece, Ireland, Portugal and Spain. Cyprus is also seeking help.[35] Why is this information germane to our discussion?

The Strings.

Any bank that loans money without tangible evidence of the borrower's ability to repay the loan, would be courting disaster. So, the ECB is within sound protocol to demand that the destitute states implement austere measures to restore a balanced budget. However, as is seen from the experience in Greece, such measures will be vigorously resisted by the general populace. But the fallout is even more severe. History has shown that when a nation experiences internal economic woes, they seek to divert the public's attention from the crisis, and perhaps repair their internal economic state simultaneously through the invasion and conquest of a weaker society. This modern Roman Empire is no different. Once more the likely target is Israel!

The Build Up.

Let us put the pieces together. Remember the Habsburgs and the Rothschilds discussed in chapter 10? The current head of the former family is Karl Habsburg, son of Otto van Habsburg. The elder Habsburg was an early advocate of the European Union, and held the position of president of the International Pan-European Union between 1973 and 2004. He has been a strong supporter of unity between the monotheistic religions of Christianity, Judaism and Islam.[36] Does that ring an End-Time bell?

The Rothschilds have influenced monetary situations and fiscal policies worldwide for over 150 years. Lately, for example, the merger of NYSE Euronext (Wall Street) with Deutsche Börse (Germany) announced February 15, 2011, heralded a further move by the Rothschilds (working behind the scenes) to control the world's economy – Deutsche Börse owning 60% and NYSE 40% of the merged companies. So then, Europe would now be positioned to control global events through the control of the world's monetary and economic systems. Although this merger faced strong opposition from the European Commission and the EU, and caused a temporary halt to the proceedings on February 2, 2012, the global control by European entities remain evident.[37] However, money is simply the springboard to effect the ultimate plan – the invasion of Israel. Can you

Personal Notes

envision the power of money in the wrong hands? It would serve to neutralize the support of Israel's allies while their enemies vigorously pursue the means of equipping their clandestine organized force for that prophetic invasion.

One may find it hard to comprehend that forces of the EU would target Israel for a preemptive attack. However, when the preceding and other factors are considered, such a perspective becomes both reasonable and feasible. For example, according to an article by Bruno Waterfield on February 18, 2009, a blueprint for the formation of the European Union's army was adopted. We are told that the army currently has 1,695,122 active personnel, and a further 2,614,491 on the Reserve list.[38] The Union's viable monetary situation has also enabled the acquisition of much arms and equipment, including several modern aircraft. Link this information to the 2010 report of the Islam Times which informed us that eight Muslims, including three women were elected to the British Parliament – demonstrating the progressive pervasiveness of the Islamic religion in Europe.[39] Then, add the observation by Adrian Michaels in The Telegraph's article dated August 8, 3009. He said *"Britain and the rest of the European Union are ignoring a demographic time bomb: a recent rush into the EU by migrants, including millions of Muslims, will change the continent beyond recognition over the next two decades, and almost no policy-makers are talking about it."* He further observed that the Muslim population had more than doubled over the last 30 years and by 2015 would have repeated that phenomenon.[40]

What can we glean from the foregoing? If Europe's population becomes predominantly Muslim, then it is reasonable to assume that the European army would also be predominantly Muslim. Add to the mix the recent threats coming out of Iran against Israel – to the extent that their ultimate desire is to see the total extermination of all Jews, and we have a ticking time bomb that will soon be detonated. At this point do you think that it is improbable for a predominantly Muslim European army to invade Israel? Can you see the subtle maneuvers made possible through the use of money?

Personal Notes

MANAGING GOD'S FINANCES

Personal Notes

It now becomes easier to relate to God's word concerning the wealth of the sinner being laid up for the just – Proverbs 13:22. I believe, more than ever before, that this is the time of the greatest transfer of wealth into the hands of those God can trust to use it for His end-time purposes. The devil and his cohorts are feverishly working at causing as much destruction before the end – money is being used as the medium. God wants us to regain that money to use for the winning of souls. If the events mentioned previously are truly indicative of the imminent return of Jesus, then money will be 'Center Stage' at this time, and it is! We need to position ourselves to receive God's benevolence. The surest way is by demonstrating our ability to manage His finances.

Conclusion

This seems to be the generation that will observe the Second Coming of Jesus – everything is in place. The main players are showing their hands – Europe being a principal vehicle. Events are occurring rapidly to usher in the anti-Christ. Climatic and other disasters are taking their toll on the economy of most nations. But churches, sensitive to the move of the Holy Spirit, are encouraging their congregants to repent for the misuse of God's finances, and therefore receive the refreshing move of the Spirit of the Lord in their financial affairs (Acts 3:19). More and more Christians are being informed about their financial heritage – the importance of money is being recognized for its true purpose. Simultaneously, we are being stirred toward a greater evangelical effort. These events are not signaling the end of the world, but rather the increased awareness of the glorious reign of our Lord, Jesus. *BUT EVEN SO, COME LORD JESUS, MARANATHA!*

MANAGING GOD'S FINANCES

Chapter 14

THE CHRISTIAN ATTITUDE TOWARD MONEY

Personal Notes

There is no getting away from it – we have been fooled. The moment Satan took possession of this world's system, he put the machinery to control its wealth into operation. Greed, avarice, and jealousy, soon led to murder and other evil traits designed to control and cement the power of evil. A hungry Esau was duped into selling his birthright for a bowl of soup – he obviously had no respect for God's order of doing things. Jacob, with the help of his mother, tricked Isaac into blessing him instead of the lawful firstborn Esau (Rebecca, knew the importance of the blessing, and respected the birthright). Laban tricked Jacob into an agreement to work an extra seven years before giving Rachael to him in marriage. In line with these economic deceptions, unsuspecting Christians were deceived into believing that it was pious to be poor. This state of affairs prevailed through the ages, to the extent that most of the earth's wealth came under the control of the unbelievers. But Believers have begun to wake up! There is a greater awareness of money, and money matters in the Christian community – our attitude toward money is changing right on time.

The Dangers.

With this new understanding we must not loose sight of the fact that everything belongs to the Lord (Psalm 24:1). Money must be seen for what it truly is – a means of exchange. We use it to obtain the goods and services that are necessary for our existence. But we must be careful not to allow greed to push money to the forefront of our lives – for the *love* of money is the root of all evil (1 Timothy 6:10). Having established that, we are now faced with the question – how do we gain the wealth without succumbing to the ever present traps which accompany the presence of money?

When we understand the full purpose of money in a Christian sense, we will see that wealth is a relative concept – it does not necessarily mean that you have a huge bank account or net worth. As Christians, we will be such great givers that money just keeps flowing toward us. We will remember that wealth in the hands of a Believer, is souls in the Kingdom of God. So, we give lavishly to world missions and evangelical work across the nation, and around the world. This means that we may not have an enormous bank account, but the sum total of our monetary gifts would establish us as those among the wealthy.

Attitudes and Actions.

In many instances our current attitude toward money is a reflection of personal decisions we made to extricate ourselves from the bonds of our childhood, cultural, and societal influences. Nevertheless, there are some who are still struggling to shake off the engrained areas of their past that are inimical to their best interests. Let us address some of them here before going further. Perhaps such a discussion may serve to free us from future bondage – it affects our very attitude toward financial matters.

There are several bad traits which can affect our lives negatively. However, we will focus on six of them mentioned by Dr. C. Thomas Anderson in his book, *"Becoming A Millionaire God's Way."* If you grew up in a home environment that was controlling, fear-based, insecure, abusive, performance oriented, or fostered hyper-responsibility, it is likely that you carried those traits into adulthood. Although each trait resulted in the development of specific attitudes, for our purpose the main observation is the avoidance of responsibility and risk. There is no way to manage God's finances effectively without acknowledging the responsibility it entails, and the risk that accompanies such responsibility. We would definitely need to change our attitudes in order to be successful.

It is possible that we may have changed our attitudes, but still lack evidence of the benefits God promised us. We therefore need to take this a step further, and employ strategies that are in line with God's directions to enable the wealth experience we desire. The following are a few approaches:

Personal Notes

Personal Notes

1. Give God first place in your life. Take care of His Church, or else you would be putting money into bags with holes. You will always be in need – working for money but can't seem to understand where it goes (Haggai 1:6).
2. You must be a tither. If you are not, and wish to benefit from God's plan, then repent and begin to tithe. It is a holy thing to God. If you simply do not understand the ramifications of this issue, some insight will be shared in a future chapter which deals with the issue exclusively – it's that important.
3. Assuming that you are a tither, your next move is to become totally debt free. The borrower is subject to the lender. Make every effort to escalate your loan repayments – use a rapid debt elimination strategy if necessary. This requires discipline.
4. Pay your bills in a timely manner. It not only saves you finance charges, but is a sign of good stewardship, and consequently the proper management of God's money – not to mention that it helps to maintain a good credit score.
5. Just give - it activates the spiritual law of reciprocity. Seek God's guidance to direct you to fertile ground where your gifts will be utilized to foster the work of the Kingdom. Remember, your bounty is established by your charity (Luke 6:38).
6. Invest. The Bible advocates it (Luke 19:12-26).
7. Diversify the investment. Do not put all your money in one place, or subscribe to one stock. The Bible gives clear directions for diversification of your investments (Ecclesiastes 11:1, 2).
8. Relax, go on a vacation, take a cruise. Enjoy the fruits of your labor. This is wisdom (Ecclesiastes 8:15).

There should be no question concerning the relevance of our attitudes toward the proper management of our financial affairs. But the crucial element at this time is our awareness of the impact of poor management, and the enhancement of the devil's work it encourages. The previous discussions on the advent of the anti-Christ, and the harnessing of wealth by those under his power, should demonstrate the imperative urgency of enabling God's transfer. The main way of doing that is through sound financial management. The rest of this book will highlight the various approaches which should result in the efficient stewardship of God's resources.

Personal Notes

MANAGING GOD'S FINANCES

Chapter 15

DECLARING MY DESTINY – VISION AND MISSION

Each of us was created for a particular purpose. Toward that end, we were each given certain gifts to aid us in the accomplishment of our individual task. All through the gospels, and to some extent the epistles, Christians are made aware that our universal task hinges around the need to draw others into the Kingdom – to evangelize. However, while some of us may actually have the gift of evangelism, there are countless others who need to utilize their primary gifts as a vehicle through which the purpose of evangelism is served. Regardless of our vocation, according to 2 Cor. 5:17-20, we are all ambassadors of Christ. If we are to manage God's finances appropriately, then we must be fully cognizant of our life's assignment. Embodied in such knowledge must be an awareness of our vision and mission.

It Begins With A Relationship

Why is it that some people seem to excel where others seem to languish? This obviously has nothing to do with the color of one's skin – people of every color thrive depending on one factor, regardless of the circumstances – their attitude. Granted, there are those who got a head start based on their inheritance. Nevertheless, if their attitude is inappropriate, they would soon lose their advantage. There is no discrimination here, Christians and non Christians alike experience the same results – the sun shines on both the just and the unjust. It is therefore imperative that we ascertain the purpose for our existence, and function within the scope compatible with the relevant goal. Only a relationship with God can channel the Christian toward his/her true individual destiny.

The question we should ask is, "Am I functioning in the role that God ordained for me?" The surest way of gaining the proper direction, is to ask the Creator! Prayer becomes the key factor in our relationship with God. There will be no lasting satisfaction in the use of our gifts outside of the God ordained plan. Once we develop a close relationship with Him, we can depend on the Holy Spirit

Personal Notes

Personal Notes

to guide us each step of the way. His guidance will include the impression of our vision, and the mission/s to experience the successful attainment of the former. This does not mean that all of us will be employed in the Church primarily, but will use our gifts to foster Kingdom relationships whatever our vocation. The proper use of our gifts will provide us with the room necessary to enjoy it. Basically, whatever we do, in whichever marketplace we are placed, our ultimate goal should be to represent the Kingdom as ambassadors.

We Are God's Representatives – First!

The thought of representing God, Creator and owner of everything that exists, is awesome. Many of us are busy working, but are we where we are supposed to be? How do we engage our assignment once it's revealed to us?

We recognize that our main task is found in our ambassadorial role for the kingdom of God. However, there are also subtasks which enable us to exist while pursuing our main function. These subtasks and our main task should be interrelated. For example, we can serve as a sanitation worker, but always have a word of encouragement and spiritual direction for those we meet from day to day. Another good example is the mailperson – what a good opportunity to share the Word with the mail! The consideration for us is the ability to channel our energy toward our goal, and not to embrace someone else's 'calling.' The latter would only serve to delay our spiritual impact on society, and to hinder our stewardship of God's resources.

Since we are representing God, then we need to ensure that we are working within His will. Psalm 143: 8, 10, gives the avenue through which we can understand which road to take every step of the way. Our individual Vision and Mission will take shape as we continue this relationship. The impetus for our strict adherence to God's directions is the unfolding of our destiny with the success of each venture we engage.

The Vision

Most of us know the familiar verse of Prov. 29:18 – *where there is no vision, the people perish* .... This is true for every aspect of life. When we plan a trip, we automatically envisage the route to get there if we are familiar with the directions. We even think of the obstacles that may be in the way. There may be unexpected detours, but we eventually arrive at our destination.

We should adopt the same attitude toward the vision given to us by God. Perseverance will be the key to overcome every challenge en-route to our destiny. This vision that is firmly entrenched in our hearts, is made easier to attain if we write it down, and formulate a statement which details the mission/s necessary to fulfill God's mandate on our lives.

Personal Notes

The Mission

Once we have that vision of our overall purpose, then the task of achieving it successfully will depend on our focus. A list of progressive steps will give us the means of ensuring we stay on track – we can always modify situations to cope with various challenges, while keeping the ultimate goal in sight. Our success lies within us. Although our desired results may not be instantaneous, we need to be persistent – God will never leave us nor forsake us. Our altitude will be based on our attitude. God has given us the tools to carry out the mission (2 Pet. 1:3, 4). What we do with those tools will determine our success or failure. In other words our management of God's resources is a key element to attain our vision.

Since this is really about doing God's work in a manner that utilizes His investment in us, then we need to pursue excellence in order to gain optimum success. A salesman when asked the secret of being the top salesman for his firm, responded, *"Every morning when I wake, I tell myself that I didn't do well the previous day, and if I didn't double my sales, I would be fired!"* Talk about motivation. It is rumored that Mahatma Gandhi once told his granddaughter that there are two kinds of people in the world – those who work, and those who take credit for the work done by others. His advice was to strive to be in the former category, since there was too much competition in the latter. The motivation for us should be a desire to please God! Our destiny is wrapped up in our obedience to God's directions and the astute stewardship of His resources. An integral part of such management is an understanding of God's laws concerning giving.

MANAGING GOD'S FINANCES

Chapter 16

THE MOTIVATION TO GIVE

Personal Notes

This entire chapter is based on my doctoral thesis with the title *"The Determinants of Giving: A Phenomenological Inquiry"* presented to Argosy University, Sarasota, Florida in December 2008, and accepted on February 9, 2009. It blends perfectly with the previous chapters, as well as those to follow.

The basic principle of managing God's finances is governed by an understanding of 'seed time and harvest.' Commonly referred to as sowing and reaping, it represents God's unique method of managing His resources toward the fulfillment of His vision and mission – His reconciliation to humankind. He makes this very clear in Genesis 8:22 – while the earth remains, there will always be seed time and harvest. Our willingness to give intelligently is therefore primary for the management of His finances. The Church, with its relationship to this vision and mission, is the main vehicle selected to accomplish this purpose. It follows that churches should therefore be aware of the dynamics which fuel and motivate people to give.

An Overview

Every nonprofit organization, including the church, depends on voluntary financial contributions for its continuous and viable existence. It is imperative as a matter of economic survival, that leaders in the church remain current with external and internal trends that could affect their fiscal viability. The psychological and sociological stimuli that motivate donors to give consistently, as well as the competitive secular attractions that help to divert contributions, all dictate the need for knowledge of donor profiles. This is necessary if the church is to adopt relevant and appropriate measures to encourage giving.

The church is unique because it is exposed to the competition presented by secular fund raising strategies, while at the same time being responsible for maintaining a theological approach that retains spiritual integrity when appealing for funds. The challenge to the church is to develop a source of income that is reliable and consistent. Invariably this responsibility is embraced by the church's membership. It seems reasonable to assume that such contributions will come from those who understand and empathize with the church's vision and mission. Toward that end many churches have sought ways and means to motivate the giving tendencies of their congregants. Generally, this is done from the pulpit through motivational sermons. However, the constant need to revisit this approach indicates that its effect is usually temporary. According to some psychologists, the need for such constant stimulation may be based on the fact that motivation is usually sustained only when individuals consider themselves an integral part of the organization – even to the extent of being part owners.

Some churches have embraced current secular marketing strategies to raise funds. There are others that continue to utilize traditional liturgical practices that are complimented by various forms of education. Many churches believe that educating the congregation is a sure way of sustaining consistent contributions. In particular, they believe that such education must include the teaching that giving is actually an act of worship. This, they advance, would have a greater impact than any motivational sermon from the pulpit. Regardless of which measure is taken, it would appear to be prudent to ascertain the motivational factors that encourage donors to give. *42*

Why Do People Give?

When it is considered that poor people give relatively as much as the wealthy, then there must be some common thread among many differences that serve as the motivating factor. While the poor are more likely to give because of their beliefs or faith, the affluent are more influenced by egocentric stimuli - what's in it for me. However both the poor and wealthy are also stimulated to give by a sense of social responsibility that supports universal human rights.

There are those who have isolated three main reasons why people give. Benevolence they contend is based on either: the warm glow derived from the pleasure of giving, because of a moral obligation, or the most significant reason - there is a relationship between the giver and recipient. The latter is known as the

Personal Notes

Personal Notes

'Matthew Effect' – where your treasure is, that's where your heart will be found.[43]

Altruism, Egoism, And Altruegoism.

At first glance a psychological approach to this question of giving reveals two main motivating factors – *altruism* and *egoism*. The former embraces the empathetic response to alleviate suffering without expecting anything in return. The latter speaks of the Law of Reciprocity – give and it shall be given back to you. In essence there can be a plethora of stimuli that motivate people to give. But there is one particular experience that can be added to the two mentioned previously – *altruegoism*. This occurs when individuals have a combination of altruistic and egoistic sentiments concerning their gifts. According to some psychologists, there is no true altruistic gift – the donor always, consciously or subconsciously, expects a return – perhaps not necessarily from the beneficiary of the gift. For example, when some of us give to the church, we do expect that God will bless us as a result of our obedience.[44]

The Cultural Impact

Giving is done in the context of social norms which are impacted by cultural mores, and the prevailing availability of relevant resources. This indicates that the benevolence of each giver can be influenced by the group to which he/she is affiliated. For example each church or denomination has its peculiar ways of worship. This determines how they each approach giving as an act of worship. Consequently, their attitude toward giving is affected by the cultural environment of their individual organizations.

One of the main observations is that churches which incorporate a focus on the Great Commission, and include relevant elements in their vision and mission, find that their congregations are more likely to be motivated toward giving. Donors are encouraged by the thought of sharing in the church's vision of accomplishing our mandated role as ambassadors for Christ.

Another cultural peculiarity within some churches is the procession to the altar to make one's financial contribution. Many Christian psychologists believe that the very culture of such an ecclesiastical environment serves as a psychological pressure that motivates participation in the procession. This suggests that the motivation inherent in the act is not solely to worship, but rather to be seen as one confirming to the obligation to bring offerings to the altar. This brings us to the final motivating factor that affects the level of contributions to the church.[45]

Personal Notes

Integrity of Purpose

There is always need for integrity in social interpersonal relationships in order to foster trust and confidence. Regardless of the cultural environment, all relationships require trust in order to enable the best efficiency. The evidence of dishonest practices which seem to envelop the corporate world has triggered distrust between the public and most organizations, including nonprofit entities such as the church. Congregants and other benefactors of the church are cognizant of the need to ensure that they receive accurate and honest disclosures concerning the program that would benefit from their benevolence. There is a lack of integrity when 90% of the contributions go toward administrative expenses, and only 10% to the actual cause, without prior disclosure to the contributors.

In the setting portrayed by the church, congregants are mindful of their responsibility to be excellent stewards of God's resources. They therefore sow lavishly when they are comfortable with the intent and purpose of the church. This is usually achieved when words from the pulpit are followed and illustrated by the evidence of successful ventures – especially when such ventures relate to the Great Commission.[46]

CONCLUSION

Churches usually base their spiritual and physical actions on their interpretation of Biblical principles. The manner in which individuals are taught, and therefore conceptualize Biblical principles related to giving, will determine the way they approach this act of worship. Some persons will be motivated to give based on Acts 20:35 which indicates that it's more of a blessing to give than to receive (altruism). Others will be motivated by the reciprocal promise contained in Luke 6:38 (egoism). But there are those who find that the two approaches are intertwined, and therefore embrace the altruegoistic concept of giving. Regardless of the motivating factor, church members must always consider that ultimately they give because of their love for God. Inherent in that love is the need to be obedient to his directions. Managing His resources efficiently displays such obedience – especially when it includes giving of the tithe.

Personal Notes

MANAGING GOD'S FINANCES

Chapter 17

TITHING – THE BASE OF GOD'S FINANCIAL PLAN

Personal Notes

There is no other financial topic that attracts as much scrutiny as tithing. Christians and non-Christians alike pose many questions concerning this discipline. The reason for such attention may be found in the fact that it deals exclusively with a commitment to give a definitive amount to the church on a consistent basis. Satan sees this as a tool that can work for or against him, and therefore fosters any deception that would serve to keep him in control of every penny. In order to avoid the pitfalls presented by an inappropriate attitude toward the tithe, Believers should ensure that they become familiar with all the rudiments surrounding this important command from God.

Almost all of the next seven chapters are reproduced partially or entirely from chapter 5 to 11 of one of my previous works, *"Discovering True Prosperity"* because it is succinct and right on point. Further knowledge gained since 2001 demanded that appropriate adjustments are made here where relevant.

It is amazing how some Christians attempt to justify their avoidance of the tithe. We each seek to enjoy the benefits of the Kingdom, but some of us would like those benefits without observing the rules. The law of the tithe is just that, a law. Like the law of gravity and other natural laws, the spiritual laws of the Kingdom work every time. Obey them and we reap the benefits, disobey them and we experience the related hardships.

This world was created perfectly by a perfect God. He was completely satisfied with His work at the end of His creative cycle (Gen. 1:31). Included in this perfect creation, were all rules and regulations necessary to govern and to ensure our enjoyment of all created things. God made everything that pertained to life and godliness available to us (2 Pet. 1:3, 4). I believe that most of us understand the existence of these rules, including the need to tithe. However, the cares of this world cause us to erect intellectual barriers in denial of that inner witness. We listen to Satan as he whispers 'Has God said?' He continually

Personal Notes

attempts to do to us as he did with Adam and Eve. We need to consider that their act of disobedience which can be considered treason, resulted in their downfall, and the suffering of all human beings who followed. They were gullible, but are we to fall for a similar ploy through lies about the tithe? The tithe is an integral aspect of our covenant with God. There is no compromise – if we neglect to tithe, we are in disobedience to God.

I have been told that in the 'Good Old days,' a man's word was his bond. This was so vital, that men defended their word with their lives. Needless to say, many men died. During the gold rush for example, prospectors got their provisions on credit based simply on their promise to pay eventually.

Now, if the word of man was treated with such respect, why don't we show a similar respect for the Word of God – the Word that offers life, and that will never fade away? The word of man changes continually, but the Word of God remains the same. God's Word and not man's, should gain our utmost loyalty.

God's word concerning tithing came with creation. Before sin, God instructed Adam concerning the only property reserved for Him alone – the Tree of the Knowledge of Good and Evil. That was Adam's perpetual tithe to God. Had he obeyed those directions, then the Tree of Live would have remained accessible to us forever (Gen. 2:16, 17)! But we disobeyed, and broke the covenant (Gen. 3:6).

Today we recognize Abraham as the father of faith. He represents the perfect example of what tithing is all about. Remember his offering to Melchizedek, King of Salem, after returning in victory from his battle with the kings (Gen. 14:18-20)? That was tithing at its best. But where did he gain this wisdom? Well, he was originally from Ur of the Chaldees, Mesopotamia. According to archaeologists, that is the cradle of civilized society. It is known that their culture embraced the tithe as a means of sustaining a viable and strong economy. Abraham had ample opportunity to experience the benefits of the system. He therefore had no reservations of tithing to the God who had already proven Himself on several occasions as a *Covenant Making, Covenant Keeping Sovereign* above all others.

Throughout the Bible we find men of God in obedience to this command to tithe. They had evidence that this covenant making God was true to His word. They found from experience that it was surely irrational to disobey Him. They found that tithing was a principal discipline which guaranteed their economic well being. In an effort to dispel Satan's lies concerning this discipline, we need to seek God's thoughts on the issue.

A Definition of The Tithe

First, let us examine the nature of the tithe. The Hebrew word for the tithe is *maasrah* – it means a tenth. The Greek goes a little further and elaborates with the word *apodekatoo*. This means to tithe as a debtor or creditor, to give, pay, or take. Note significantly that this implies that someone owns the tithe. According to Leviticus 27:30 – 32, the tithe is the tenth part (10%) of all *new increases*, nothing less. Moreover it is owned by God and therefore holy.

Material increases in Old Testament times, and to a lesser extent in the New, were based on livestock and agricultural produce. Today we have substituted such things with a simpler means of exchange, money. We should therefore generally tithe from our financial increases.

It should be noted that the tithe represents the bare minimum of our return to God. It is not enough to be considered exorbitant, but adequate enough to be recognized as a sacrifice. Anything less than the tithe, given in substitution of the tithe, is indicative of a lack of knowledge or worse, a disregard for God's sovereignty.

Who Owns the Tithe?

Who really owns this money that we protect with a passion? Psalm 24:1 and Haggai 2:5-9, tell us that the earth and everything within belong to the Lord, including the silver and gold. We, like Adam, are His stewards, and must be mindful to ensure that we manage His finances according to His rules. He gave us this responsibility from the beginning when He commanded us in Gen. 1:26 to

Personal Notes

take dominion over the earth and its contents. When we refuse to obey God's directions concerning giving, we are attempting to deprive Him of what is rightfully His!

Personal Notes

Tithing is a Command

Simply put, we tithe for two main reasons, because it's a command from God (Mal. 3:10) and because we love Him (1 John 2:1-5). When we withhold the tithe because of a perceived lack of integrity, or confidence in man's sincerity, we miss the essence of who is really in control. If we truly believe that God is omniscient, and omnipotent, then we must accept that our obedience to His command will cause us to reap the benefits which He promised in Mal. 3. This is, despite any misuse by those entrusted as stewards of His tithe – they have to answer to Him, not us. We do not stop driving because others misuse the roads, and sometimes drive while under the influence of alcohol. We continue to drive, but remain vigilant in order to avoid such accidents. History is replete with the judgment meted out to those who betray God's trust as stewards of the tithe. Remember, it's holy unto God – we tithe to Him, not to the pastor.

Is The Tithe Required Today?

Many of us, in an attempt to avoid the tithe, have ignored Jesus' total accomplishment through the Cross. We have incorrectly confined the tithe to the Old Testament era. One of the most common responses when asked about the relevance of the tithe to contemporary liturgical observances is that the tithe came under the Law, and died with it at the Cross. There are several reasons to refute such observations.

In the first place, the tithe was instituted before the Law. The Law came through Moses after he served to deliver Israel from Egypt. Israel spent 430 years in Egypt. Their forefathers Abraham, Isaac, and Jacob were all tithers. Tithing as we know it was therefore in existence at least 430 years before the Law was given to Moses at Sinai. A look at Hebrews 7:1-17 demonstrates that tithing is a bona fide observation of our worship to Jesus as our High Priest – He receives tithes from us to honor God, in the same way Melchizedek received tithes from

Personal Notes

Abraham. According to Heb. 6:15 and Gal. 3:13, 14, 29, we are Abraham's seed through Jesus, and therefore obligated to maintain the covenant with all its concomitant rules, including the need to tithe.

Is it from The Net or Gross?

There has been various teachings on how the tithe should be calculated – should it be taken from our Gross or net earnings? This should really be a simple issue. If we examined our pay stubs, we would notice that our taxes to the Federal and State governments were calculated from our gross wages. We had no discretionary power to regulate this situation. Should God be shown any less respect because He allows us the freedom to make our contributions voluntarily? Any increase in wages we receive is not added to the net, but to the gross for tax purposes. The tithe which represents all new increases, should be calculated from the gross. The motto should be 'Render unto Uncle Sam what's his, and unto God what's His' (Matt. 22:21). We could never be greater givers than God.

The Storehouse

Many Christians, divide their tithe between several churches. Mal. 3:10 directs us to bring *all* the tithe into the storehouse. The storehouse is actually the central place where we are fed the Word of God – our home church. If you say that the gospel is free, you are correct. But note, it takes money to spread it. If we are moved to give to other churches, then we must do so by giving an offering beyond the tithe. The whole tithe goes to our local church body.

God's House Comes First

Have you ever wondered where all the money you earned went? It seems as though you are working just to fill a financial void which seems to have no bottom. Haggai 1:4-11 explains it. When we neglect God's house and take care of our own without respect to His, we indeed put our wages into a bag with holes. The tithe should be our first consideration when we receive our wages. According to Ps. 34:22, we would never be desolate once we trust God. We should tithe in faith, believing God – without faith it's impossible to please Him (Heb. 11:6). Our faithful diligence will result in a just reward as we give God first place in our lives.

Personal Notes

How Should We Give?

We should note that when God accused non-tithers of robbing Him, He indicated that He was robbed of tithes and offerings (Mal. 3:8). This signifies that there is a difference between the two. The tithe, as mentioned previously, is the tenth part of all new increases. The offering is any amount in excess of the tithe. While the tithe must go to the home church in the whole, the offering can be given to any church body for the furtherance of the gospel. Our attitude in giving is of paramount importance. We should give cheerfully, willingly, lovingly, and with gratitude for the opportunity to be a part of God's financial plan (2 Cor. 9:7, 11, 12; 8:12, 24). Our motives should be pure (Mat. 6:2-4).

Finally, we should understand that God's purpose for the tithe includes the provision for His ministers – enabling them to pursue His work without any distractions because of secular needs (Num. 18:21-28). When we contribute to the house of God, we also help to prevent the poor and widows from being destitute (Deut. 14:27-29; 26:12-19). Our love for God should cause us to honor Him with our giving (Prov. 3:9, 10). This is really a tool of financial management that enables us to reap the benefits of the Kingdom.

The resources of this world are limited – God's resources are unlimited. Which economy would you rather trust? The world's economy filled with its man made scarcity and shortages promises us nothing. God's Kingdom economy has more than enough for us all. This discipline, although a command from God, is the only invitation to test Him. On the other hand, it also tests our obedience, and our ability to manage His resources. Our next step should therefore embody a plan of our own to ensure that we remain loyal to our obligation.[47]

MANAGING GOD'S FINANCES

Chapter 18

GOOD STEWARDSHIP – BUDGETING AS A TOOL

Personal Notes

Many of our financial ills are caused by our failure to plan seriously. Oh we try to plan all right, but it's mainly a head thing without the detailed approach which dictates a commitment to paper. We are operating as irresponsible stewards of God's funds when we spend without the discipline that budgeting demands. What then are the requirements for a proper budget?

Let Us Bake A Cake

What kind of cake shall we bake? Some people prefer chocolate, others vanilla, while some won't leave a fruit cake alone. But regardless of which type we agree to bake, there are certain common essentials – basic ingredients which every cake must have. Well this may be our first attempt at such a challenging venture. If we are to get it right, we must follow a ***PLAN. Principle # 1 – A Budget is a plan.***

Getting Started

Since we may wish to repeat this process on another occasion, it would be a good idea to document each step. This will also help to ensure accuracy, and to make adjustments as necessary if modification is needed. ***Principle # 2 – Document each step.***

Now that we have a pencil and pad, let us list everything that we think would be needed for a complete cake. A good method to adopt here would be to treat this like a story – it has a beginning, a middle, and an end. If we think systematically of all the ingredients needed, and the process required, we should be able to tabulate all the essentials necessary to complete our project.

It should be easy for us to list the obvious things such as flour, sugar, butter, fruits etc. But we sometimes forget the little things such as salt and baking soda. That's why documenting the process is so crucial.

Principle # 3 – Price each item. We need to know how much money to set aside to complete the cake. So we obtain the current prices for each ingredient,

Personal Notes

and add an extra amount in case of any contingency related to the price, or unforeseen costs associated with the venture.

Principle # 4 – Ensure there is enough money to complete the cake. Do not force the issue. If we do not have enough money to meet the cost for the cake, then we either postpone our adventure, or scale down the size of the cake to accommodate the amount of money we have.

Principle # 5 – Keep within the price range. In order to avoid exhausting our funds before all ingredients are acquired, we need to monitor each purchase to ensure that we remain within the price range allocated in our plan.

Mixing and Baking

The mixing is easy. We follow the instructions from the recipe we received from Aunt Bakit. We set the oven at the appropriate temperature, and lovingly fill the baking pans with the mixture. Finally, as the temperature is attained, we place the pans into the oven. The aroma is tantalizing – we can hardly wait to sample the fruit of our labor.

Counting The Cost

After what seems like a lifetime, the cake is done. We anxiously take a knife, and ever so delicately, remove a slice. Surprise! Surprise! It tastes better than we thought it would. While enjoying the delicious flavor, we begin thinking of a similar venture in the near future. And so we reflect on the cost to complete this one.

When we check our documented list, we are satisfied that we accurately accounted for every ingredient and related cost. Wherever prices differed from our original list, we had made the relevant adjustments. Planning this event was a breeze. Now we know how much it should cost to bake a cake. Or do we?

This is the area that most persons omit, and it can be crucial to the success of any enterprise – counting the overhead costs. For example, we never considered that a portion of our water rates was included when we used water to mix the dough. Nor did we take into account the gas or electrical cost for the actual baking. What about the gasoline we utilized to get to the store for the

Personal Notes

ingredients? Although this may seem over simplified, yet at another level such omissions can be financially disastrous. ***Principle # 6 – Always review the plan, and include all details with a cost, however insignificant.***

In A Nutshell

Simply put, a budget is a written detailed plan which attaches a cost to every item related to a particular venture. It seeks to relate the total cost to the actual funds available for expenditure. This serves to avoid over expenditure, and to maintain a healthy and stable financial environment.

The same principles involved in baking a cake are applicable to budgeting for any other situation. However, there are some peculiarities for a regular budget that are designed to control living expenses:

1. Ascertain your source of income and the amount. Include your salary, gifts, and Income Tax refunds to name a few.
2. You should know how much you spend, and on what. Your check book can be a good source for such information. If this situation is vague, then you will need to log all your expenditure for the next three months. Divide the total by three to arrive at your average monthly expenditure. If your check book is accurate, then list each item for the last year, month by month, and total them under individual categories. This serves to indicate how much you spend on each item annually.
3. Make a realistic monthly budget to cover all your expenses based on the information from your actions above. The total should not be greater than your income mentioned at item 1.
4. Ensure that your budget includes your tithes and personal savings.

CONCLUSION

Proper stewardship is an indication of sound management. God demands this essential attribute of those who are entrusted with His property. If we are incapable of managing our own, how can God trust us with more of His?

MANAGING GOD'S FINANCES

Improper management causes money to sound the warning knell of disaster – poverty. Budgeting is as easy as baking a cake. The exercise is well worth it, and will save us from experiencing the words of Prov. 24:33, 34. Who wants poverty to overtake them like an armed man? If you are serious about being debt free, then budgeting is a must. Let us glorify God through wise management of our financial affairs – it's really His money!

Personal Notes

MANAGING GOD'S FINANCES

Chapter 19

IDENTIFYING AND REPAIRING BAD DEBT

Personal Notes

Once more I reproduce from my previous work *"Discovering True Prosperity."* The American economy, to a large extent, is based on a credit system. Everything and anything can be had on credit! Our existence in the business world revolves around our credit worthiness. We therefore strive to remain in good standing by paying our bills promptly. But is this God's best for us? I think not! Recent experiences have shown how the credit system can lead to entrepreneurial greed, and to the subsequent demise of those who use it for irrational self aggrandizement. As Christians we should pay strict attention to Deut. 28:12 which advocates a position to lend, and not to borrow. Further, according to Deut. 23:19, 20, we can lend with the expectation of receiving interest on the loan, providing the loan is not to another Believer. In other words, we should profit from the credit system instead of being victims.

Most of us desire to be on the benevolent side of the Kingdom's principles. However, various circumstances have placed us in the uncomfortable position of the penalty box. Week after week, paycheck after paycheck, we come short of satisfying our financial commitment fully. We keep juggling our expenses until there is no more room for maneuver. What do we do then – that is, apart from praying? Well, fortunately, there are various answers to such a dilemma. I have selected the following mainly because I have personally traveled this route successfully. Assuming that you are a faithful tither, then:

1. Examine your position with personal honesty. Ask yourself the question – How did I get to this point?
2. Stop purchasing on credit. Stop doing anything that got you into the predicament.
3. Make a list of all outstanding bills. Identify:
   a. Their individual due dates.

Personal Notes

b. Whether they are short term (one year or less), long term (over one year), or continuous, such as utility bills.

4. Make a list of all income.
5. Compare the totals of 3 and 4 above.
6. If 4 is greater than 3, praise the Lord. If not, thank Him for the wisdom to navigate towards that end.

Now you are able to assess your financial position objectively.

First Things First

Businesses lean heavily on computers to retain client information, and to generate invoices and reports. Computers do what they are told, and respond automatically without variation. If the due date on your bill is the first day of each month, any failure to pay at that time will result in a relative response from the computer. Your credit rating could be severely hampered in this way. I have found that by simply communicating with the creditor, and seeking an extension to pay, usually circumvents any uncomfortable experiences. You avoid repeated phone calls from the company, and also save your credit rating – not to mention that it's the courteous thing to do.

Debt In The Midst of Plenty

What do we do if we discover that our income *is greater* than our expenses, yet we continually experience hardships each month? This would suggest one of several things, or a combination of some such as:

1. We do not prepare monthly budgets – there is no plan for our expenditure.
2. We spend compulsively on items not in our budget (if we have one) without checking first to ensure that we could afford the additional expenditure. This is known as *Oniomania (shopaholicism)* by psychologists.
3. We do not save from each pay period.

This is indicative of a lack of discipline, or worse, a blatant disregard for our financial commitments. Such an attitude only helps to foster the agenda of those outside of the Kingdom. We end up paying them *avoidable* interest and revenue. This is foolish action. According to Prov. 11:29, those who are wise will profit from our folly.

Obviously, if we are serious about becoming debt free, then the recognition of this personal problem should lead to a change in attitude. We should now begin to prepare regular financial plans (budgets), spending extra only after ascertaining that there would be no negative impact on our financial position. We would also ensure tat a set amount is channeled regularly to our savings account. But there is also a spiritual side to this situation, as we shall see later.

No Way Out!

In many instances we find ourselves in an untenable financial position because of bad decisions. But sometimes things happen beyond our control. For example, unexpected vehicular repairs, or a leak in the roof, or a broken boiler. This sudden, and additional expenditure can have far reaching consequences if we did not plan for contingencies – a saving plan to cover emergencies. In the absence of an alternate source to pay an unexpected bill, we can end up juggling our monthly payments, and progressively become tardy with some of them. This starts the cycle of the negative impact of 'The Acceptable Minimum' – penalties for late payments increase our indebtedness.

Regardless of how we arrived at our present position, our desire is to be debt free. What can we do in the circumstances – it seems hopeless! We have no alternative source of income, and our costs are rising monthly. Well, take heart, you are a part of a majority. There are various methods that can alleviate such situations. However, each has its individual merits and demerits. They should each be examined carefully on an individual basis before being utilized:

1. Cutting out the fat.
2. Consolidating outstanding bills.
3. The Collections strategy.
4. Rapid Repayment Strategy

Personal Notes

MANAGING GOD'S FINANCES

Personal Notes

At this point it would be wise to reexamine ourselves. Once more the question is, do we really wish to be debt free? If so, are we prepared to exercise the necessary discipline required, and to be committed to the methods adopted? If the answers are in the affirmative, then we should be ready to proceed.

Let us establish immediately that there is a spirit of debt! His task is to drive us toward the compulsive and irrational spending habits that result in unnecessary indebtedness. Our first task is to bind that spirit, and banish it from our financial affairs. You can use the following declaration, or choose words of your own. Speak with authority, "***In the name of Jesus, I bind you spirit of debt, and cast you away from me and all my financial affairs. I command you to loose me, and to release my finances immediately, in the name of Jesus. I now embrace God's ways in handling my finances.***" Now we are ready to begin a step by step approach toward our financial freedom.

Cutting Out The Fat

Before we broke free from the spirit of debt, we purchased compulsively. We now need to make a list of all our monthly expenditure. Ensure that our costs are as accurate as possible. Next we identify those items from the list that we can do without. Total their value. In many instances we will find that the total cost represents a bill that went unpaid. We strike such items from our budget. After this exercise, if our expenses are still greater than our income, we need to go to the next level. We may possess many items which we seldom or never use. If they have retained a market value, we should sell them. The revenue may assist us to pay off an entire debt. Perhaps these actions are still insufficient to bring our expenses below our income. What next?

Consolidating Our Outstanding Debt

We need to be careful here. This can work against our plan to be debt free. The system operates by lowering our overall monthly repayments, while in most instances increasing the duration of the repayment term. The crucial element here is the interest rate. ***If it is less than the average of our existing rates combined, then it is a viable option.*** Remember, borrowing is not evil if the proceeds work

Personal Notes

in your favor. In this case you are positioning yourself to save monthly late fees by obtaining a manageable monthly repayment schedule. If the new monthly repayment is low enough, we may be able to retain the original remaining duration of our outstanding debt. This will require an increase in the new monthly payment.

The Collections Strategy

When we fail to pay our monthly bills consistently, creditors sell the debt to collection agencies for less than the outstanding balance. Then the harassment begins. There are those who take advantage of such a system. They utilize this very strategy by collection agencies to 'help' us get rid of the debt. These debt free consultants advise us to stop paying our monthly commitment to the creditor, but redirect the money to them instead. They then keep our payments in an escrow account. When the original creditor sells our debt to a collections agency, the debt consultant then negotiates with that agency. This way they are able to reduce our outstanding debt to a fraction of the original amount. They then use the escrow amount and add any shortfall to pay the collections agency.

We are now committed to pay the debt free consultant the new remaining balance on our debt. It sounds like a good strategy. However the negative impact is the effect on our credit score. The consultant is quick to point out that with timely payment to them, our credit is soon repaired. One needs to weigh such a program very carefully before accepting the proposal from a debt free consultant.

Rapid Repayment Strategy

The preceding actions may have been inadequate to cover some of our outstanding bills – there are bills that may remain ineligible for consolidation. This is usually the case when their interest rate is lower than that offered for the consolidation of our debt. Remember we spoke about the need to communicate with our creditors? Well, one of the things we can suggest during our discussion is to make lower monthly payments. However, we must be prepared to offer a sound plan to clear the debt ultimately.

Personal Notes

Suppose for example, we had a monthly household income of $4,000.00, with normal recurring expenses such as groceries and utilities of $3,100.00. If we also had other bills with a total minimum payment of $1,300.00, then we would not have sufficient funds to cover this latter expense – the remaining balance after recurring expense would only be $900.00. In such a situation we would calculate our suggested lower monthly payments as follows:

a. Total monthly household income	$4,000.00
b. Less total monthly recurring expenses	-$3,100.00
c. Balance remaining for other bills	$ 900.00
d. Divide c by the total monthly minimum payments	÷ $1,300.00
e. The percentage of each bill we could afford to pay	.69

Note that we need to find a way to bury our tithes within the recurring expenses – most creditors will not accept the tithe as a bona fide recurring expense.

Below is a breakdown of what the suggested minimum payment should be for each outstanding bill:

Item	Present Payment	%	New Payment
1. Car	$ 300.00	X.69	$207.00
2. Credit Card	$ 50.00	X.69	$ 34.50
3. Student Loan	$ 150.00	X.69	$103.50
4. Medical	$ 200.00	X.69	$138.00
5. Consumer Cards	$ 200.00	X.69	$138.00
6. Credit Union	$ 150.00	X.69	$103.50
7. Finance Company	$ 250.00	X.69	$172.50
Total	$1,300.00		$897.00

The driving force behind this plan is that there is no discriminatory treatment to any of the creditors – all receive a similar percentage of the original monthly minimum payment. The plan is a clear indication of our willingness to pay, and demonstrates the ability to satisfy the full repayment over time. Once we show each creditor such a plan, it is likely that they will accept – particularly because of the sound assessment and the evidence that we were making a genuine

Personal Notes

effort to honor our obligations. This reduced payment schedule is affordable, and enables us to avoid penalties. It also opens the door to explore the possibility of repaying each debt earlier than originally anticipated.

The next phase is to list each outstanding bill in a special format – the smallest at the top and the largest at the bottom. We then endeavor to pay a little extra on the first bill on our list – even if it's just the $3.00 remaining after we pay our new monthly minimum. ***Note that our monthly payment to each creditor must remain timely, and that we should not incur any new credit!*** As soon as the first bill is repaid, we should add that monthly payment to the minimum payment of the second bill on our list. This will result in the escalated repayment of this second bill. We follow the same pattern with the third bill when the second is fully repaid, and do the same for all subsequent bills on our list. By now you can see the tremendous power focused on eradicating our outstanding debt. This will eliminate a number of years from the original schedule, and can save us a bundle in interest payments, depending on the size of the original loan or credit.

There is a word of caution if we include our mortgage repayment in this strategy. We must ensure that each payment is timely. We must also indicate quite clearly that any sum in excess of the required monthly payment should be credited to the principal. This serves to reduce the principal balance, and hence the total interest - shaving years off the term of the mortgage loan. Failure to make this stipulation can result in the company crediting the interest or an escrow account instead. That would certainly defeat our purpose for the extra payment. Whatever our actions are, we should not lose focus on the Biblical principles that will see us through every step of the way.

Expect A Miracle

Once you have followed the foregoing directions in a disciplined manner, then you would have demonstrated to God that you were capable of managing His finances, and that you were serious about your commitment to be debt free. You have given Him something to work with. The next step is a leap of faith – help someone else to come out of debt! What? Yes, it's Biblical. Even though you are in debt, assisting someone in a similar situation releases Kingdom energy in your favor. Several scriptures support such actions – Eph.6:8; Mat. 7:12; and Gal. 6:7 are a few. You choose where you will plant the seed. It could be with a relative or friend, or your church. But like our previous actions, there must be a disciplined structure here as well.

The power within the rapid repayment strategy is the additional payment amount available for the next bill once the previous is paid in full. Rather than adding this full amount to the next bill, we should reserve 10% to assist in clearing the debt of our chosen beneficiary. The remaining 90% goes as the monthly addition to the bill we intend to pay off rapidly. This 10%, 90% division should be an ongoing process until all outstanding bills are paid in full. You would be assisting someone else to repay their debt rapidly as well.[48]

Remember the widow and her sons in 2 Kings 4: 1-7? The creditors were about to take her sons in lieu of an outstanding debt. But because her family was a God faring one, God worked through Elisha to create a miracle. The little oil that she had miraculously increased to a flow that enabled her to sell enough to clear her debt. But note verse 7 – she had enough remaining to sustain her family after clearing the debt, and to avoid a recurrence of the original problem. God brings no sorrow with His promises. What He did before, He is certainly capable and willing to repeat. Will you trust Him?

A Good Report

So far we have identified and made steps to eradicate bad debt. However, we need to engage a final step to ensure that we remain in good standing with the financial community. Since our credit worthiness is crucial in enabling us to take full advantage of this economic system, we must maintain a good credit report.

The first step on our road to recovery, is to obtain a current copy of our credit report. This can be achieved by paying a fee to one of the credit agencies, or by requesting a free copy from the last agency that gave a report that resulted in the denial of credit – they are legally obligated by Federal Law to honor the request. This report should be checked for accuracy. Any discrepancies should be

Personal Notes

disputed immediately with the creditor, and cleared. Another report should be obtained after six months into your rapid repayment schedule. This should serve as encouragement, but be careful to avoid the temptation of using this good credit to engage new debt.

Most creditors seek credit information for the last six months, a few others for one year. However, requests for large loans such as a mortgage, can result in deeper credit checks. It follows that our faithful and disciplined commitment to repay our debt will soon help us to regain a credible report. Now we are poised to embark on the next phase of managing God's finances intelligently.[48]

Personal Notes

Chapter 20

SPIRITUAL AND NATURAL INVESTMENTS

Personal Notes

Many Christians shy away from making any investment in the economic market. There can be several reasons for this attitude, including fear. But Jesus Himself made it quite clear that sound investment practices should be the goal of every Believer (Mat. 25:14-30). It is evident that our ability to engage this aspect of financial management will depend to a large extent on our own economic situation. That's why, if our position is untenable, we need to observe the direction contained in the previous chapter. Once we have discretionary funds, then intelligent investments should follow.

In the beginning, the creation of this natural world flowed from God's spiritual existence. Everything that is established by a firm foundation owes its origin to a spiritual orientation. The success or failure of our economic endeavors is no exception. If we are to engage in sound investments, we need to acknowledge this concept, and therefore examine our spiritual awareness prior to any natural venture.

The Spiritual

Much of what is chronicled here is based on my observations when writing *"Discovering True Prosperity."* We have already established that God has no aversion to entrepreneurship, in fact, He encourages it. However, there are particular rules and guidelines that must be observed if we are to maximize our potential economic viability. We must position ourselves spiritually in order to receive God's blessings in the natural. How do we accomplish that? The following are three basic steps:

1. We must observe the Law of the Tithe.
2. We must sow seeds.
3. We must meditate constantly on the Word of God.

Personal Notes

The Law of The Tithe

This law cannot be overemphasized. Once we fail to obey this command, we must be willing to accept failure in our economic activities. To some, the temporary success in a venture may cause a denial of the truth. But we each realize sooner or later that as a non-tither, our foundation is insecure. It is presumptuous to neglect the tithe, yet expect the very God whom we disobey to shower us with blessings! Tithing is the key that turns the ignition on our economic vehicle. The very act releases a spiritual reaction which guarantees our success. The next activity is understood clearly if we think of farming.

Sowing Seeds

So much negative things have been said concerning this topic, that many Christians remain confused, or skeptical about its truth. But if we focus our attention on the Word of God, we would soon be assured of God's plan for us through this medium. God wishes us to prosper, and has instituted certain laws for our benefit. According to Gen. 8:22, there will always be a need to plant seeds, and a time to reap a harvest. Luke 6:38 guides us to the law of reciprocity, while Gal. 6:7, 8 points out that we will reap whatever we sow. These are laws just like gravity, they will not change – they represent cause and effect. These laws are etched in eternity – an integral part of the words of God's covenant with us. God cannot, and will not lie. As we sow seeds – give of our substance, we compliment the key of the tithe. Our giving acts like the pressure of our feet on the accelerator of our economic vehicle which was already started and in gear through the tithe.

We find that as we engage these principles, we are actually creating a heavenly bank account according to Matt. 6:19-21. This spiritual account is insulated against the effects of the natural economic mood swings such as shortages and surpluses. It remains steady in growth as we adhere to the governing Kingdom principle.

This heavenly account is now available for our withdrawals when needed. There is no account number to submit for access to funds. All that is necessary is the simple compliance with the rules set by the bank's President, Jehovah. For

Personal Notes

example, according to 1 John 5:14, 15, we must ensure that we seek withdrawals based on His will. Both 1 John 3:21, 22 and James 4:3 highlight the need for integrity of purpose if our requests are to be honored. There is no doubt that God intends that we should enjoy this life – right here and now. It is the purity of our approach that will dictate the level of our success.

Meditating on the Word

The bible represents the manual that contains all the directions for our spiritual and natural growth. In the same way that we expect the manual for a new device to guide us through its assembly and functions, we should also rely on the Bible to guide us through life. Some of these guidelines can be found in Joshua 1:8; Deut. 11:18-20; Prov. 1:28-32; and Psalms 112:1, 3.

The observance of these guidelines triggers a reciprocal spiritual action which results in the enhancement of our spiritual awareness, growth, and development. God is careful and very explicit in His directions to us. He indicates causes and effects, actions and reactions, as well as rewards and penalties. The bottom line is that the choice is ours. We choose whom we will follow. For example, Prov. 1:32 above warns us that those who amass wealth contrary to God's principles, will experience destructive elements in their affairs. Conversely, according to Psalms 112:1, 3, obedience to God's commands leads to wealth and riches.

The natural result of meditating on God's Word is that it becomes flesh, and manifests itself in our affairs (dwells among us). The focus on the Word pertaining to prosperity for the *whole man* – spirit, soul, and body, causes us to benefit in those areas. Our purity of thought, devoid of the lusts of the flesh, clears the channel for God's benevolence toward us. Joseph, son of Jacob, is a perfect example of how this works. Examine his life as illustrated in Gen. chapters 39 – 47.

Jacob must have obeyed Deut. 11:18-20, the Word was engrained in his son. Joseph was sold into slavery by his own brothers, yet he remained faithful to the God he served. His words were always based on his allegiance, and on the

Personal Notes

promises of the covenant. He found favor with the Egyptian authorities regardless of where he was placed: In his master's house he became the head slave. In prison he became the head prisoner. Brought before Pharaoh to interpret his dreams, he soon established his wisdom and became governor of the land. Note that it was God who supplied him with the necessary ideas and insights. In like manner, innovative plans and directions will be divinely imparted to us for our benefit and His glory, as we diligently observe His Word. God will direct us to financial wealth for our well being, and to accomplish His purposes for the rest of humanity.

It is imperative that we understand the importance of our spiritual walk with God. This enables us to recognize that it's the wisest investment we could ever make. Everything else springs from this association with our Savior. We must first observe the spiritual, then the natural falls into place as an inevitable consequence.

The Natural

This spiritual relationship with God has now become a way of life. Various ideas of enrichment begin to flow. We are each provisioned with individual gifts and talents. The ideas lead us to focus on appropriate areas where the gifts could be optimized. But don't be surprised if God places us in unfamiliar territory – His ways are higher than ours, and He never fails. Our trust and confidence in God is of paramount importance when implementing spiritual insights into natural circumstances. That's why our spiritual association with God is so crucial – we need to be assured that our spiritual directions are from Him. Regardless of our individual areas of expertise, God has a plan for our success.

An Overview of The Natural

Natural investments can encompass various forms, all of which may be summarized as follows:

1. Savings Accounts – Prov. 6:6-8.
2. Real Estate – Acts 4:36, 37.
3. Entrepreneurship – 1 Thess. 4:11, 12; Rom. 12:11.

4. The Stock Market – Matt. 25:14-29.

It should be observed however, that each method has its own guidelines to recognize risks, maximize rewards, embrace or avoid challenges, and to minimize the incidence of failure. The decisions we make should be based on the signals we receive from each venture, as well as the applicable Word of God which justifies each action. Remember, the ultimate goal of all our business activities should be to glorify Jesus.

The areas of enterprise mentioned above are not the only disciplines available, but were chosen because they each encompass other disciplines, and affect each of us in some way. If we are active participants, then we help to shape the lives of others. On the other hand, if we are passive, then those who are active serve to shape our lives. You may find this a difficult concept to embrace. How can my regular savings account impact the lives of others, you may ask? Well, just think of all the loans the banks issue to students to help with their tuition, loans to purchase cars, houses, and other goods and services. Whose money do you think they invest? Ours of course. So, indirectly we are assisting others to attain their individual goals. At a higher level, the banks make loans to foreign countries in need. Again, where do you think the money comes from? It's ours!

The same observation holds true for each of the other ventures. Real Estate provides accommodation for tenants while affording us remuneration for our efforts. Entrepreneurship generates goods and services to others in various forms, while rewarding us for exercising sound business practices. The Stock Market, a peculiar discipline, touches every life on this earth, and gives us a return on our investment commensurate with our level of risk and patience. It's like the ecological system – everything is interrelated, plants, animals, and their various habitats. Our God is the Ultimate Genius – His creation follows the pattern of His perfection. Let us examine the selected natural investments and their links to the spiritual a bit further.

Personal Notes

The savings Account

Proverbs 6:6-8 advises us of the need to save in preparation for the lean times. Every working person should set aside a portion of their wages as savings. The guideline is to save at least 5% of our regular income. Depending on individual circumstances, we should have the equivalent of three to six months of our usual expenses available for use in emergencies. This makes us somewhat self sufficient, and obviates the need to borrow on interest in times of difficulty.

This is as basic as we can get. The regular savings account is the safest enterprise with a return on our investment. But because of that very safety, it is the least rewarding. Most banks gave less than 1 % interest on our savings, but use our money to grant loans at an interest of 4% or more. Nevertheless, it is wise to do something, even if this is the only level we could afford – our commitment would soon help to change the situation. If you need another scriptural reference that covers the prudence and wisdom of saving, as well as illustrates the benefits of following God's plan, read the story of Joseph in Genesis 41:25 – 47:26.

Joseph saved an entire nation and others, including his estranged family, by storing grain during the times of plenty. When the famine came, he had enough to supply even 'foreigners.' Note his dealings with his own brothers – he took no money from them, although they were willing to pay for the supplies. At the conclusion of the famine, he had economically enslaved all the Egyptians for Pharaoh's personal aggrandizement. Obviously, he also benefited as a result.

The question that remains at this point is, what do we do with our money after attaining the financial reserve of three to six months in our savings account? There is no one answer to this question. Our actions will be guided by factors such as our goals, age, talent, gifts, and marital status, to name a few. Perhaps we wish to remain simple and to follow the trend depicted by our savings investments. The two favorite options available in this case are, Time Deposits – better known as CDs, and the Money Market Account. The latter is preferable because of its flexibility and potential to generate a greater return. The retention of any amount beyond our emergency reserve, should take into account other

Personal Notes

forms of investment, bearing in mind that the ultimate goal should be to help support God's financial plan for the Church. This is as safe as it gets. All other ventures involve some degree of risk.

Personal Notes

Real Estate Investments

This is one of the better practices. Our involvement can be passive or active. The former can be illustrated by our ownership of a multi-family dwelling in which we utilize one section as our personal residence, while renting out the remainder. Apart from maintenance and repairs, our participation is minimal.

There are others who pursue Real Estate investment as a progressive business venture. They buy and sell property, or retain each new acquisition for rental purposes. Whichever is chosen, specific knowledge of the discipline is necessary, and personal business acumen desirable. This too is a relatively safe endeavor. The beauty lies in the fact that real estate property almost always appreciates – its value continues to rise over time. The current down turn is really an anomaly that will eventually adjust itself. If you have the means, the knowledge, and the patience, this can be a very lucrative venture. Once more we need to remember our covenant with God. Like Barnabas, a land owner, we should use our assets to assist the Church whenever the opportunity presents itself (Acts 4:36, 37).

The Entrepreneur

The essential element of all our transactions is the development of a close relationship with our God. Once this is consistent, and we meditate on His Word regularly, we are sure to gain uncommon insight into areas God wishes to channel toward us. Successful entrepreneurial undertakings are always first heralded by brilliant ideas. There is a bit of this discipline in each of us, but many of us are discouraged through fear of the unknown. An anointed entrepreneur casts fear aside, and implements the ideas God imparts. It is our meditation that paves the way for our successful efforts – the Word which we meditate on is manifested in the fruit of the ideas we implement.

Personal Notes

It is most assured that the world will hasten to our doors as we build a better mousetrap. But sometimes the fear of getting our hands caught in the mechanism of the trap, prevents us from building the device. Remember, what one can conceive, one can achieve. God Himself declared that truth in Gen. 11:6. Fear, the opposite of faith, is our worst enemy. But our meditation should lead us to acknowledge that God did not give us a spirit of fear, but rather deposited a spirit of love, power, and a sound mind within us (2 Tim. 1:7). We may be reticent because of the inherent risk involved, but we should remember that God is in charge.

Do you have the ability to be an entrepreneur? Have you been flooded with ideas which you never implemented? If you meet the spiritual criteria mentioned previously, you may be wasting ideas that God initiated to bless you. Reject timidity, embrace God's directions with boldness. The Church and perhaps the world are awaiting your impact. Let this sobering thought remain with you – the richest place in all the earth is the cemetery – it contains the greatest volume of unrealized ideas that had unlimited economic potential for the owners!

The Stock Market

"Wall Street runs the world!" What a statement. But it's technically true in worldly affairs. Just reflect on the recent financial issues triggered by the market, and their effect on the various economies of the world. Activity in the stock market influences interest rates, and therefore everything else. Because of this dynamic personality, the stock market represents one of the most lucrative avenues for successful investments.

There are two influential factors that can affect our success or failure – fear and greed. The former prevents us from entering lucrative arrangements because of the risk, while the latter propels us to seek greater returns without regard for the consequences. Both extremes are inadvisable as children of God who are mandated to manage His resources intelligently. The following are a few guidelines for dealing in the 'Market.'

MANAGING GOD'S FINANCES

Personal Notes

The Market comprises of various stocks and devices which carry diverse degrees of risk. The catch here is that the more risk involved, greater is the return on the investment. How then should one conduct business in such an environment? Here again, our age has an influence on our decision – the older we are, the more averse we become to risk – we develop a 'Risk Tolerance Level.' Depending on how involved we wish to be personally, will also help to determine how we invest. The hands on investor monitors his investment regularly, and makes spontaneous adjustments as he/she sees fit. The individual who simply recognizes the potential for a greater return in the Market, may just allow his investments to work for him with infrequent modifications.

Whichever way is chosen, there are certain basic observations:

1. Risk is always present, but should not be feared.
2. Frequent movement of investments can increase returns, but also serve as the greatest avenue for potential loss.
3. A wise portfolio is a diversified one.
4. Remaining with a diversified portfolio for the long haul has the greatest potential for the greatest returns on investments.
5. It is better to risk than to retain idle funds. Money is currency, and should be allowed to flow – money is meant to work for us.

Most persons would ask – what is a portfolio/? The simple answer is that it's a group of stocks or other devices owned by an individual for investment purposes. The next question is likely to be – What's a diversified portfolio? Think of owning shares in several companies – companies A, B, C, D, E, F, and G. Each of them has a different degree of risk associated with the Market. Depending on one's Risk Tolerance Level – how much risk we would feel comfortable with, we would invest more in the riskier items and less in the safer areas, or vice versa. But the general idea would be to spread our investments among various types of items e.g., oil, telecommunications, electronics, agriculture, entertainment, sports, and steel. Once we remain with this *diversified* group for the long term, our experience would be a balanced outcome yielding an overall profit. This result is

Personal Notes

based on the Market's peculiar behavior – when some items in our portfolio lose revenue, because of the diversification, others will most likely gain a profit which should serve to offset the loss.

Trading on the Market has evolved to the extent that we now are able to handle our portfolio directly over the Internet without the help of a broker. But we must be careful here since a knowledge of market behavior is crucial to our success. It is better to seek expert advice if there is any doubt about your ability to organize this activity. But whatever you do, do not sit on the sidelines, get involved.

One of the better investments is the 401K. This is usually offered through employers. Some employers even match your investment as an incentive for you to save toward your retirement. This investment is attractive because contributions are deducted from your salary before taxes, leaving a greater amount as take home pay. At retirement, when the withdrawal of these savings is taxable, you would most likely be in a lower tax bracket. This allows you to save more then, than if the same funds were taxed progressively over the years prior to retirement if you were not contributing to the 401K. Another way to save further at retirement, is to roll the proceeds of the 401K over to an annuity. This allows you to receive a set sum annually, and only that amount is taxed at the time it's received, rather than the lump sum if you had not rolled it over. Icing on the cake is that you would continue to gain interest on the balance remaining in the annuity after you receive the designated sum annually.

The parable told by Jesus in Matt. 25:14-21, 24-27, touches on the rewards for risk versus the penalties for fear. ***God advises that we engage in the business practice that best suits our gifts and talents.*** Our diligence is sure to reap a just reward. Managing God's resources efficiently calls not only for sound business acumen, but more importantly on a relationship with Him. Without an understanding and engagement of the spiritual, the natural will become laborious and difficult to manipulate in our favor, and to the glory of God.*49*

MANAGING GOD'S FINANCES

Chapter 21

RETIREMENT PLANNING – WILLS AND TRUSTS

The year is 1945. Everyone is making an effort to return to normalcy after a harsh war. Soldiers are rejoining their families with the joy that freedom brings. Everyone is hilariously happy. Nine months later, many of these same people are even more ecstatic as they welcome new additions to their families. There is an unprecedented escalation of births all over the country. The "Baby Boom" has arrived.

But it's not until much later that social experts realize the potential impact of this unusual situation on the economy. It is now believed that the Social Security Administration will not have enough funds to cope with the required expenditure when those 'babies' retire. That means in another few years from now, unless some positive action is taken, the Social Security fund will be bankrupt. Consequently, since we should not depend on expected benefits from Social Security, we need to make adequate provision now for our retirement.

Putting It Together

This is almost similar to making a budget. If we do not intend to work for others for the rest of our lives, then we must create a retirement plan now. The earlier we put such a plan into effect, the easier it is to attain our goal. We need to know where we are in order to get to where we wish to be. The first step is therefore to ascertain our ***net worth*** so we can recognize our current financial position, and therefore the best strategy to move toward our intended goal. The easiest way to do this is to multiply our annual pre-tax salary by our age, and then divide the result by ten. If the plan involves a couple, then use the age of the older person. At age 40, with an annual salary of $75,000.00, the equation would be; Net Worth = $75,000.00 X 40/10. The result, $300,000.00, is what our current net worth *should* be. The next step in the exercise is to find out our *actual* net worth.

Your actual net worth is simply identifying the financial value of the things you own and the debt you owe. It is really a grand total of all your assets

Personal Notes

minus your liabilities. The following steps should aid you in making the calculations:

1. List the current market value of all your large assets first – including the home and vehicles.
2. List other assets such as the balance in your checking and savings accounts, cash, investments, 401K, and other retirement accounts.
3. Don't forget assets such as the Grand piano, jewelry, computers – anything with a value above $300. You can enter their estimated value as a lump sum.
4. The total value of the items from item 1 to 3 represents the total of all your assets.
5. The next step is to catalog your outstanding liabilities – what you owe creditors – start with the largest debt, including the balance on your mortgage, student loans, and car loans. Make a separate list of loans such as consumer and credit cards.
6. Finally, total all of your outstanding liabilities – go through the list to ensure that you have covered all your debt.
7. You are now in a position to subtract your total liabilities from the total of your assets. The result is your *current* net worth.

Since you know your goal for retirement, and what your current net worth should be, as well as what it really is, you can see whether you are on track, or if there is a shortfall. Most of us will experience the latter. But having the knowledge positions us to take necessary steps to correct the situation.[53]

There are several questions embodied in the creation of a viable retirement plan. Before we arrive at our final calculations, we should have answered at least the following four questions:

1. What kind of lifestyle do we desire at retirement?
2. How much would it cost in today's dollars to live that lifestyle?

Personal Notes

3. Taking inflation into consideration, what would the cost be at the time of my retirement?
4. What do I need to save now on a monthly or annual basis in order to have the funds I will need at retirement?

The answers to those questions represent the essence of retirement planning. There are various financial vehicles available to help us attain our goal. However, we need to be selective, since not all have a Christian base.

A Godly Approach

Many of us enjoy a pension scheme on our jobs. We also have the 401K which is categorized as a Deferred Compensation Plan. Our first action should be to find out how much each of these would be worth at our retirement. Your Benefits Clerk should be able to assist in this regard. Next we combine the retirement value of these accounts with the retirement value of any other financial investments we may have – including the Individual Retirement Account (IRA), Credit Union savings and such. When we total these amounts if they are not equal to, or more than enough to meet our desired financial goal, then we need to make some adjustments.

Here is where the directions of a trusted financial adviser should be of immense value to our retirement strategy. Depending on our age, a mistake can be very costly – the older we are, the more difficult it is to correct financial errors. Below are a few items you may wish to consider:

1. Do you have any Life Insurance, and if so, is it the kind that can benefit you at retirement?
2. Is your insurance coverage for your life and home adequate? Too much can be a misuse of funds, while too little can be dangerous. A conservative estimate is that your Life Insurance should be equivalent to five times your annual salary before taxes.
3. Can your IRA, 401K or any other investment be rolled over to another account (preferably an annuity) at retirement?

Personal Notes

Personal Notes

4. What about the impact of Income Taxes on your savings at retirement? Have you invested in such a way as to minimize your Income tax liability when you retire?
5. How do you stand with risk? The younger you are, the greater should be your tolerance for risk. This diminishes as you grow older. In any case, it's Biblical to invest (Luke 19:12-26). Just remember to diversify your investments – spread them among stocks, bonds of various risk levels, noting that the greater risk brings the greater reward. However, putting everything on high risk items because of the high return, is a sign of greed rather than wisdom. A diversified spread will prove advantageous in the long term (Eccl. 11:1, 2).

Wills and Living Trusts

This can be a very complex area to plan, and may or may not need the guidance of an attorney. Nevertheless there are some basic guidelines for each that can help to determine whether professional help is advisable.

Most individuals wish to ensure that after their death, their estate is distributed in a manner commensurate with their personal preferences. The Will and the Living Trust are devices that can help to achieve this goal. There are advantages and disadvantages for each. However, it's your individual circumstances that should serve to guide your choice. The following shows some comparisons that can help to influence the situation:

1. The Will needs to be probated, and this is required separately for property which is held out-of-state. The Living Trust does not need to be probated, and therefore avoids the costs associated with out-of- state property as well.
2. Court supervision monitors any challenges from creditors or beneficiaries of the Will. There is no automatic supervision for disputes to the Living trust.
3. Estate taxes for the Will and Living trust are similar.

4. Whereas a Will requires the use of a Power-of- Attorney or conservator to manage your assets, the Living trust allows you to manage your assets providing you are capable of doing so.
5. It costs relatively less to prepare a Will than it does for a Living Trust – there are differences in complexities.
6. A will becomes public information after your death, while the Living trust continues to be private.

The purpose of the Will is to allow you to indicate how you would like your estate distributed after your death. It gives you the scope to designate which aspect of your property should go to particular beneficiaries. In order to achieve this, you need to appoint a trusted person as the Executor of your Will. Finally, if you have minor children, a Will would allow you to choose their guardian. Note that if you die without a Will – that is, if you die intestate, the state and the court will make those decisions on your behalf.

The Living Trust is operable during your life. It is a revocable instrument which allows you to make adjustments as you see fit. It is one of the safest vehicles to ensure that the distribution of your assets is done according to your desire. The creation of a Trust also ensures that your financial affairs continue to be managed if you become incapacitated, as well as after your death. This instrument remains private, and safeguards the integrity of your intent for your property.

CONCLUSION

There is no way that every aspect of retirement planning could be covered by this presentation. However, enough was shared at least to help you assess your current position. It would be a travesty for any hard working individual to discover that they need to work beyond retirement in order to maintain a comfortable standard of living. It is also untenable that your wishes for the distribution of your assets would be ignored. The fact that you are a Christian does not obviate the need to plan. God's goodness to you *now* is to enable you to

Personal Notes

relax *later.* This can only be achieved through sound management of the resources He entrusts to you.

Personal Notes

MANAGING GOD'S FINANCES

Chapter 22

THE ROLE OF SPIRITUAL GIFTS

The management of God's finances suggests that we have finances to manage. The acquisition of this 'wealth' is actually connected to the gifts that God, in His wisdom, and for His purpose, bestowed upon us individually. These gifts represent the hub around which all our successful activities thrive.

Every Believer is a minister – God is our ultimate employer. Our worldly employers recognize the need to equip us with the necessary tools to perform our tasks. In like manner, God ensures that we have the spiritual gifts necessary to accomplish His goals.[1]

God's benevolence to us has a purpose – it's the empowerment that enables us to help others. The ideas for development, the experience of fulfillment, and the joy of service, are all fueled by the use of various spiritual gifts. This wealth that we manage then, is really God's method of ensuring that the entire package of spiritual gifts, our discipline, and faithfulness, serve the purpose for the End-Time 'Harvest of Souls.'

Talents and Gifts

We are each born with at least one talent. Some of us are artistic, others are writers, some excel at sports, while the academic arena comes naturally to the selected few. But whatever the talent may be, it should not be confused with the Spiritual Gifts of God – they are not the same. Whereas a Spiritual gift may enhance the use of a talent, the talent has no influence on the use of a Spiritual gift. A good example is the talent to teach. An excellent secular teacher may find it difficult to teach a Sunday School class, that is, unless 'gifted' to do so – the Word of God is spiritually discerned!

A gift of the Spirit is an impartation given only to Believers. This impartation comes when we accept the Holy Spirit as our Helper. Many Christians remain skeptical about this miracle. However, once embraced, we find ourselves functioning at a higher level without a full comprehension of the

Personal Notes

transformation. It is really God equipping us for service. It follows that we need to understand the different purposes of the Spiritual gifts so that our full cooperation comes easy, and therefore yields the utmost benefits.

Personal Notes

The Role of the Holy Spirit

Peter was a fisherman, Jesus was not. Yet, when he obeyed the Spirit filled Jesus, and cast his net where previously there had been no fish, he gained an exceptional catch (Luke 5:4 – 6). He could then readily understand how Jesus could make him a fisher of men. Despite his talent to fish, he had to follow the instructions to remain in Jerusalem until he was endued with power from on high – only then would he be successful at catching men. His obedience launched him into a new and exciting dimension. He was bold before, but brash. Now, with the presence of the Holy Spirit in his live, he remained bold, but relinquished the brashness, while adding a polished and eloquent approach to his service. This change was so dramatic, that even the learned Pharisees and Sadducees were perplexed. The presence of the Spirit of God made the difference (Acts 1:4, 8; 2:3, 4, 40, 41).

When we accepted Jesus as our Savior, the Holy Spirit took residence within us – our bodies are temples of the Holy Spirit (1 Cor. 6:19, 20). With this event also comes all the fruit of the Spirit – Love, joy, peace etc. (Gal. 5:22, 23). This enables us to relate to God and to each other on a different plain. However, there is another level of spiritual development that can be obtained simultaneously with, or subsequent to the 'New Birth.' It's this second touch of the Spirit that brings with it the gifts necessary for service. When Philip preached in Samaria, many were saved, but it took a subsequent act by the apostles to ensure that they received this special infilling of the Holy Spirit (Acts 8:14-17).

Jesus was baptized by John the Baptist, then afterwards, the Spirit of God descended upon Him and drove Him into the wilderness. It was only after this episode that He started His ministry and demonstrated the various gifts with awesome results (Luke 4:18, 19). This special baptism is a necessary prerequisite if we are to function in the gifts of the Spirit (Mark 1:9-11).

MANAGING GOD'S FINANCES

Personal Notes

The Spiritual Gifts

There are three main categories of Spiritual gifts: Motivational, Ministerial, and the gifts of Manifestation. These gifts have their individual peculiarities and functions. However, they are interrelated at various levels to complete the works of God.

Motivational Gifts

According to the Book of Romans chapter 12 and verses 6 – 8, we are given different gifts based on the grace of God. But each of us needs to utilize faith and diligence to operate with the gift bestowed on us individually. There are particular traits that help to identify the functional gifts in our lives.

What gives you an impulsive urge to speak words of edification at every opportunity, or to help someone in difficulty, or to instruct others correctly in some discipline or action? What makes you want to pull someone to the side to give them words of encouragement? What leads you to give, and give, and to give? Why can't you stand to see things disorganized, but move speedily to put them in order – even when it's none of your business? Why do you extend a helping hand to someone who seemingly is unworthy of such help? If you can answer any of these questions, you may already know what Motivational gift you possess. Yes, these are illustrations of the way Motivational gifts propel you into action.

Each Believer has at least one Motivational gift. It is imperative that we each know what that gift is. Such knowledge should prevent us from attempting to function in areas for which we are not equipped. When we operate in the individual capacity according to God's plan, we maximize efficiency and avoid confusion and conflict. Perhaps a hypothetical scenario would help to illustrate these seven gifts with greater clarity.

Try to visualize the following scene: Seven persons were invited to a special meeting on a very hot day. Six of them were punctual. The seventh person, Mary, while experiencing the heat of the day, thought it a good idea to surprise her colleagues with some ice cream – the gift of **Giving**. She was tardy because she made the stop to purchase the ice cream.

Personal Notes

Mary pushed the door to the *carpeted* office, both hands full with the delectable condiment. At the same time, Tom was attempting to retrieve a pen which had fallen behind the door. You guessed it. There was a clash, and the ice cream tumbled unto the carpet, some also spilling unto Tom's clothing. The various reactions of each person tell the story of their individual gifts.

Tom was livid. He told Mary that she should have knocked before entering – oblivious to the fact that her hands were both occupied with the ice cream. He then began to caution her for future reference – 'You should seek help whenever carrying such burdens' he said – **Exhortation**. Meanwhile, Mary was distraught because her surprise had failed, and she had no money to replace the ice cream (forget Tom's pants and the soiled carpet!) – **Giving**. Bill, another member of the team, had already gone to the phone to arrange the shampooing of the carpet by the building's management. He was now seeking assistance to move the large conference table in anticipation of the cleaning effort – **Administration**. By this time, Jane had returned with a bucket and a mop, and began to remove the liquid from the carpet. She had already used napkins in an effort to remove 'stuff' from Tom's clothing – **Service**. Veronica meanwhile, was consoling the distraught Mary – 'It could have happened to anyone, don't worry about it,' she contributed – **Mercy**. Beverly observed all the commotion then remarked, 'I knew something was about to happen when Tom leaned over and the door opened. Well, the ice cream seems a good idea. We should replace it' – **Prophecy.** Trevor, another observer, finally had his say. He began to relate his various experiences with stained carpets, and the best way to restore them to pristine condition – **Teaching**. Which character best depicts you?

Ministry Gifts

It was mentioned at the beginning of this discussion that every Believer is a minister. However, not every Believer is called to function in the Ministerial Gifts mentioned in Eph. 4:11, 12. These gifts are specially allocated as God wills.

Personal Notes

It should be noted that individuals anointed for the offices of the Ministerial Gifts, are also able to, and should use the Gifts of the other categories. Each apostle, prophet, evangelist, pastor or teacher, should recognize their Motivational gifts, and be ready to be used by the Spirit of God in the Gifts of Manifestation as He wills.

Gifts of Manifestation

According to 1 Cor. 12:7-11, these gifts are distributed to Spirit filled Believers as the Spirit wills. A different one of these nine gifts can be evident at different times through the same believer. But only Jesus had the full measure of the Spirit, and therefore experienced all nine operating throughout His ministry.

A careful examination of the text reveals that these Gifts can be subdivided into three distinct categories. Norman Robertson in his book "The Supernatural Church," identified them as follows:

Revelation Gifts *(The Eyes of God):*

a. A Word of Wisdom.
b. A Word of Knowledge
c. Discerning of spirits.

Power/Demonstrating Gifts *(The Hand of God):*

a. Special Faith.
b. Gifts of Healings.
c. Working of Miracles.

Vocal/Inspiration Gifts *(The Mouth of God):*

a. Prophecy.
b. Kinds of Tongues.
c. Interpretation of Tongues.[51]

Every Believer should be acquainted with these Spiritual Gifts and the way they function. They are mentioned here because of their importance for a successful experience in our assignments and ministry. We should be aware of the association. However, we should also be aware that this topic has a wider scope than illustrated in this limited discourse.

MANAGING GOD'S FINANCES

The Connection to Financial Management

You may have noticed that some effort was made to elaborate on the Motivational Gifts. This is so because of their connection to our individual assignments. When we experience prosperity for the whole man, spirit, soul, and body, we gain spiritual insight into the tasks before us. More directly, the person who has the Motivational Gift of Giving, for example, may discover that entrepreneurship and philanthropy are attractive, and easily accomplished. The Teacher will serve to educate others, helping them to break the poverty cycle. The Administrator may organize groups for missions of evangelism. The scope is limitless. But it does not end here.

As we utilize our Motivational Gifts to carry out our assignments, we must always be cognizant of the Gifts of Manifestation. These will also propel us into bolder activity with the assurance of great success. Supernatural Faith, for example, fills us with a resilience borne by an unexplainable confidence. We move into areas which previously eluded us, principally because of fear.

Regardless of the gifts we utilize, the experience is success after success, once they are used according to God's will. Since our gifts will make room for us, it is likely that we will experience a constant flow of finances, and consequently the need to manage such wealth efficiently.

The interrelationship and functioning of these Gifts differ from individual to individual. It's the Holy Spirit who works in, and through us to help others. Such help to others would be forthcoming only if we managed God's resources effectively – both the Gifts, as well as the finances they help to generate. Therefore, to the extent that we acknowledge the work and purpose of the Holy Spirit in our lives, and express such awareness through the use of the Gifts, we would be satisfying God's mandate to us for the rest of the world.[50]

Personal Notes

MANAGING GOD'S FINANCES

Chapter 23

EMPLOYING THE WEALTH – GOD'S REDEMPTIVE PLAN

It should be obvious from the various discussions so far, that God intends to use His resources to redeem a lost world. You and I are the instruments. But one may ask, "What is the actual plan in these final days?" Now that Jesus has already paid the price on Calvary, what else remains to be accomplished, and how?

We are reminded that Jesus will not return until the Gospel is preached all over the earth. By now we realize that it will take enormous sums of money to achieve this goal. It is reasonable to assume, therefore, that God has made the necessary arrangements for this final push. I believe that the time is at hand. If we are to play a role in God's plan of redemption, then we have already determined to take the contents of this book seriously. It is evident that there must be a transference of wealth to enable the funding of this End-Time harvest of souls. Our faithful management of God's resources will afford an easier transition which is imminent. The following observations should help us to retain a focused perspective:

01. We must acknowledge that the earth is the Lord's, and the fullness thereof, the world and all they that dwell therein (Ps. 24:1).

02. Since it all belongs to God, it would be unwise to attempt to rob Him of His tithes. We are cursed if we do (Mal. 3:8-11).

03. Failure to attend to God's House will result in a never ending cycle of 'not enough.' It would be like putting our wages into a bag with holes (Hagg. 1:6).

04. But God's desire for us is the same as Paul's was for Gaius – that we should experience

Personal Notes

prosperity and good health, even as our souls prosper (3 John 2).

05. That's why we are advised to meditate on the Word day and night. Our souls will definitely prosper, and so would every other area of our lives (Josh. 1:8).

06. Because God wants us to prosper, once we obey His Word, He will supply all of our needs (Phil. 4:19).

07. Why? Because He wants us to owe no man anything, but love. We need to be debt free if we are to be as effective as God wants us to be in taking the Gospel to the world (Rom. 13:8).

08. So, through His genius He provides a way for us to obtain wealth – by giving, we activate the spiritual law of reciprocity (Luke 6:38).

09. He will flood us with ideas as He directs us to regain the wealth Adam lost to the sinner. We regain that wealth in order to redistribute it – to our children's children, to evangelical work, and to other areas that He may indicate from time to time (Prov. 13:22).

10. But when we come into this wealth, we must remember that it is God who gives us this power. We must also remember that He gives us this wealth to establish His covenant (Deut. 8:18).

11. Herein lies the final crux of His plan for the redemption of the world. The covenant to be established was made with Abraham. It

Personal Notes

Personal Notes

stipulated that through him all families of the earth would be blessed (Gen. 12:3).

12. But Abraham is no longer here, and all families of the earth have not been blessed with a knowledge of the Word. Since God's Word is true and never fails, who then will accomplish this task? According to Gal. 3:29 we are Abraham's seed through Christ. It seems therefore that we are the ones who have inherited this covenant task. It is through us that God's plan of redemption will finally reach the ends of the earth. Yes, the wealth He blesses us with is not to be lavished on ourselves, but rather to take care of our immediate needs, and to use the surplus to help fund the End-Time harvest of souls.

13. Assuming that we are tithers, even as we obey God in this End-Time venture, all the blessings mentioned in Deut. 28:1-14, will flow through the open windows of Heaven as promised in Mal. 3:10.

14. At the end, our obedience, our faithful management of His resources, will position us to hear the Lord declare, "Well done thou good and faithful servant" (Matt. 25:21).

Chapter 23

Personal Notes

That's what this is all about! In the final analysis, our true purpose is to glorify God by doing His will. Jesus in His final words to us before ascending into Heaven, commanded us to go into all the world, and to preach the Gospel to all creatures (Mark 16:15). Let us take Him at His word – let us strive to be debt free, and to appropriate and manage the wealth necessary to fund the task of sharing the good news of God's redemptive sacrifice on Calvary. Then we could wrap up this whole evangelical outreach in a jiffy, and go on Home to Glory. ***Even so, come dear Lord Jesus – Maranatha!***

Personal Notes

MANAGING GOD'S FINANCES

Chapter 24

THE ROLE OF THE HOLY SPIRIT – NOW

Personal Notes

The power of Pentecost did not end on that faithful day when 120 disciples of Jesus were baptized by the Holy Spirit. It was rather the beginning of the 'Last Days,' according to the word. The power of the Holy Spirit is still evident in the Church today. But is there any difference to His operations today when compared to early Jewish and Christian experiences? Several worldwide developments would suggest that there is.

In chapter 12 we discussed various areas of operation in which it was evident that the Holy Spirit influenced actions and outcomes. At that time Israel (the Fig Tree) was used as a model for our edification. The Holy Spirit served as their guide through anointed men and women of God. We saw that when they obeyed His directions, there was prosperity - spirit, soul, and body. Conversely, when they disobeyed, they found themselves on the precipice of disaster. In C.E. 70, after the assault by the Romans, and destruction of the temple (predicted by Jesus, Mark 13:1, 2) Israel was dispersed, and became the Diaspora of God's chosen people. They did not become a nation again until 1948. During this time it has been the gentile Christians who have been carrying the banner of Christ, and effecting God's plan of reconciliation.

The confusion subtly engineered by Satan, has caused great dissension among various members of the Christian Body. Arguments concerning the viability of the tithe, the baptism of the Holy Spirit, the need to give frequently to the Church, all play a role in retarding the proper management of God's resources. If individuals recognize the role of finances in this End-Time move, then many of the fears and reticence would be dispelled. So, since the Word of God is true, how is the Holy Spirit defeating Satan's devices such as corruption and other forms of monetary control?

MANAGING GOD'S FINANCES

Chapter 24

Personal Notes

Changing with The Times

God does not change – He's the same today as He was yesterday, and will be the same tomorrow. However, He changes *us* in order that we might confirm to His image. The changes in society over time dictate a change in our attitudes toward the progressive control of various systems. Our change is facilitated by the presence of the Holy Spirit in our lives. The climatic anomalies, the escalating earthquakes of significant magnitude worldwide, the volcanic eruptions in unlikely places, wars, and the economic distress of powerful nations such as the United States, all indicate that God is bringing closure to this phase of His redemptive work (Matt. 24: 1-51). How should Believers cooperate with the Holy Spirit *now?*

Since the Holy Spirit will not change, it follows that the same sound Biblical principles He instilled in us will work in today's world. However, He continues to impress in our hearts the urgency of the current situation to bring loved ones and others into the Kingdom. Managing His finances effectively is one sure way of serving this purpose. Let's relate this statement to current world monetary affairs.

The United States Economy

By now everyone knows that we are in trouble. Despite aggressive and innovative economic methods, there is still some concern for our revival. As mentioned earlier, the problem has been fueled by greed and a credit system that ignored the basic principles of sound financial management. The issue for us as Christians is this – there has never been a greater opportunity in recent times where individuals could take advantage of such low interest rates. The housing market with an unprecedented number of foreclosures is one of the primary targets. But are we positioned to maximize this opportunity? Did we listen to the Holy Spirit when He used various men and women to direct us toward freedom from debt? If we did, then we can have money work for us instead of us working for money!

Personal Notes

The impact of this economic down turn was not restricted to this nation – what happened on Wall Street sent economic ripples throughout the world. Japan, England, and more recently Greece, have introduced methods to stem the tide from becoming an economic Tsunami. Yet the latter had to be bailed out with an initial loan of $58 billion dollars from the European Union. This situation with Greece highlights the core of End-Time prophecy and the need for Christians to be vigilant in their management of resources, while keeping an eye on the global significance of recent developments. Spirit filled Believers are monitoring this situation.

Greece and the European Union

It was mentioned earlier that three significant developments occurred in 1948 – Israel became a nation once more, the World Council of Churches was formed, and the European Union had it's inaugural meeting. It is this latter event that now takes center stage. Between 1948 and now, the European Union has created an army, and directly related to our discussion, the introduction of the Eurodollar. Now, in the current crisis, most countries prefer to deal in Eurodollars rather than American. This is an important observation because he who controls the wealth, controls the world. The stipulations Greece was forced to agree with before being granted the loan is indicative of the power being exercised by the European Union. Other European nations such as Ireland, Portugal, and Spain, have also received bailout loans, based on the same austere requirements from the ECB.

If it's true (and I believe it is) that the anti-Christ will emerge through the European Union, and if the European Union gains control of the economies of member nations and others through loans, then we can easily see the resurgence of the Roman Empire once more as prophesied in Daniel chapter 7:1-12 *(I believe the lion represents Britain, the Eagle's Wings which are removed, represent the USA, the Bear represents Russia, the Leopard represents Germany, and the Beast with iron teeth represents the creation of the new Roman Empire. Relate this to the ten toes of the beast mentioned in Daniel chapter 2, a mixture of clay and iron*

Personal Notes

also signifying the resurgence of the Roman Empire). Link that possibility to a strong assumption that there was an agreement between Yasser Arafat of the PLO and the European nations in Russia before he died, and the current nuclear threats of Iran focused on Israel, what do we have? We have a stage set for the invasion of Israel! By the Spirit of God, this is a viable scenario that should not be taken lightly.

What Should Christians Do?

There are three suggested options open to Believers at this time – all three are proactive and include both a spiritual and natural perspective. The first two options depend on our financial position. If you are in debt, then follow the instructions in chapter 19 to extricate yourself from financial bondage speedily. If you are already debt free, then chapter 20 should give you some guidelines to manage the resources entrusted to you. In the final analysis we all need to position ourselves for the transference of wealth through careful and efficient financial maneuvers. In both instances the voice of the Holy Spirit should be an audible prompt in every decision. The only way to be assured of this is to embrace the third option – develop a relationship with Him through prayer.

The need for prayer cannot be overemphasized. Prayer that's centered on faith based on the Word will bring results. How should we pray? Meditate on the Word that is applicable to your particular situation. Ask the Holy Spirit to bring fresh revelation concerning the spiritual and natural routes you should adopt. This is made easier when you keep abreast of current economic trends – praying will help you to avoid the various pitfalls of the secular world. The power of the Holy Spirit will take up the slack where you *seem* powerless.

CONCLUSION

Through it all, from the beginning of creation to the present time, the Holy Spirit has orchestrated events that will lead back to the Garden of Eden at a point before sin came into the world. In every phase, the management of God's resources has played a crucial role in keeping the plan of reconciliation on track. This book has chronicled various examples in different eras. The idea is to demonstrate how sound financial management by Believers could foster the move of the Spirit to draw others into the Kingdom.

To the extent that you have made a firm decision to follow the guidance of the Holy Spirit in the management of God's finances, then this work was successful. The only remaining criterion for us to enjoy this earthly existence fully, is to exercise love one to the other so that the rest of the world would be convinced that Jesus is real (John 13:34, 35). It is not about riches, it's not about wealth in itself. It's about our love for Jesus, and our fellow human beings, using wisdom to deploy the wealth in the ministry of reconciliation. Even so, come Lord Jesus. Amen.

Personal Notes

MANAGING GOD'S FINANCES

Notes

01. Vision – *The Origin of Evil* – Page 1.

02. MacArthur, John – *The Origin of Evil* – Page 9.

03. Nurse, Donald A. – *Discovering True Prosperity – Pages 36-39.*

04. Conner & Malmin – *The Covenant – Page 69.*

05-24. Knox, John Jay – *A History of Banking in the United States* – Pages 2, 3, 4, 9, 26, 27, 29, 32, 82, 17, 19, 80, 85 and 86.

25-29. Church, J.R. – *Guardian of the Grail* – Pages 26, 63, 193, 203, and 204.

30-33. Van Impe, Jack – Perhaps Today – Sep/Oct 1995 Page 2; Nov/Dec 1995, Page 2.

34. Lewis, Michael – *Touring the ruins of the Old Economy* – New York Times (2011-09-26).

35. *The Economist (April 29, 2010).* Acropolis Now.

36. *The New York Times (1988-10-16).* Headliners; Papal Audience.

37. *New York Stock Exchange (2012-03-01).* Press Release.

38. Waterfield, Bruno. *Blueprint for EU army to be agreed.* The Daily Telegraph (London, 2010-05-12).

39. *English Islam Times (9 May 2010).* Eight Muslims in British Parliament.

40. Michaels, Adrian (2009-08-08). *Muslim Europe: the demographic time bomb transforming our continent.* The Telegraph.

41. Kennedy, Helen (2010-05-06). *Huge protests break out as Greece approves drastic budget cuts.* New York Daily News.

42. Nurse, Donald A. *The Determinants of Giving: A Phenomenological Inquiry* – Pages 2, 3, 30, 41, 42, 44, 46.

43. Nurse, Donald A. *The Determinants of Giving: A Phenomenological inquiry* – Page 31.

44. Nurse, Donald A. *The Determinants of Giving: A Phenomenological Inquiry* – Pages 106, 107.

45. Nurse, Donald A. *The Determinants of Giving: A Phenomenological Inquiry* – Pages 109, 110, 111.

46. Nurse, Donald A. *The Determinants of Giving: A Phenomenological Inquiry* – Pages 56, 57.

47. Nurse, Donald A. *Discovering True Prosperity.* Pages 50-58.

48. Nurse, Donald A. *Discovering True Prosperity.* Pages 60-72.

49. Nurse, Donald A. *Discovering True Prosperity.* Pages 73-88.

50. Nurse, Donald A. *Discovering true Prosperity*. Pages 90-98.

51. Robertson, Norman. *The Supernatural Church.* Page 48.

52. Anderson, Thomas C. *Becoming A Millionaire God's Way.* Pages 17-20.

53. Anderson, Thomas C. *Becoming A Millionaire God's Way.* Pages 15, 16.

MANAGING GOD'S FINANCES

Bibliography

Anderson, Thomas C. *Becoming A Millionaire God's Way.* (2004). Winwood Publishing Inc., Mesa, Arizona.

Church, J.R. *Guardian of The Grail* (1991). Prophecy Publications.

Conner, K & Malmin, K. *The Covenant (1983).* Bible Temple Publishing, Portland, Oregon.

Ellis, Albert. *Overcoming Destructive Beliefs, Feelings, and Behaviors (2001).* Prometheus Books, Amherst, New York.

Kennedy, Helen (2010-05-06). *Huge protests break out as Greece approves drastic budget cuts.* New York Daily News. Retrieved on 9/3/2012 from http://articles.nydailynews.com/2010-05-06/news/27063733_1_drastic-budget-cuts-parliament-building-greece.

Knox, John Jay, (Assisted by a Corp of financial writers in the various States). *The History of Banking in The United States (1903).* Bradford Rhodes And Company, New York.

Lewis, Michael (2011-09-26). *Touring the Ruins of the Old Economy.* Retrieved on 06/06/2012 from http://www.nytimes.com/2011/09/27/books/boomerang-by-michael-lewis-review.html.

MacArthur, John. *The Origin of Evil (2000).* Extracted on February 17, 2010 from http://www.biblebb.com/files/MAC/90-235.htm.

Michaels, Adrian (2009-08-08). *Muslim Europe: the demographic time bomb transforming our continent.* Retrieved on 3/1/2012 from http://www.telegraph.co.uk/news/worldnews/europe/5994047/muslim-Europe-the-demographic-time-bomb-transforming-our-continent.html.

Nurse, Donald A. *The Determinants of Giving: A Phenomenological Inquiry (2009).* Argosy University, Sarasota, Florida.

Nurse, Donald A. *Discovering True Prosperity (2001).* Abundant Life Center New Jersey, USA.

Robertson, Norman. *The Supernatural Church (1993).* NRM Publications, Charlotte, North Carolina.

The Economist (April 29, 2010). *Acropolis Now.* Retrieved on 6/22/2011 from http://www.economist.com/node/16009099.

The Islam Times (May 9, 2010). *Eight Muslims in British parliament.* Retrieved on 8/30/2012 from http://www.islamtimes.org/vdcip5ar.t1aw2lict.html

The New York Stock Exchange (2012-03-01). *Press Release.* Retrieved 3/1/2012 from http://www.nyse.com/press/1328178461772.html.

The New York Times (1988-10-16). *Headliners; Papal Audience.* Retrieved on 05/05/2010 from http://query.nytimes.com/gst/fullpage.html?res=940DE7DC1630F935A25753C1A96E948260.

Van Impe, Jack. *Perhaps Today*. Sep/Oct & Nov/Dec 1995.

Vision (Winter 2000). The origin of Evil. Extracted on February 17, 2010 from http://www.vision.org/visionmedia/article.aspx?id=1053

Waterfield, Bruno (2009-02-18). *Blueprint for EU army to be agreed.* Retrieved on 05/12/2010 from http://www.telegraph.co.uk/news/worldnews/europe/eu/4689736/Blueprint-for-EU-army-to-be-agreed.html.